TALES *from the* BALLPARK

TALES *from the* BALLPARK

More of the Greatest
True Baseball Stories Ever Told

MIKE SHANNON *author of* Tales from the Dugout

CB
CONTEMPORARY BOOKS

Library of Congress Cataloging-in-Publication Data

Shannon, Mike.
    Tales from the ballpark : more of the greatest true baseball
stories ever told / Mike Shannon.
        p.   cm. — (Baseball tales)
    Includes index.
    ISBN 0-8092-2771-1
    1. Baseball—United States—Anecdotes.   2. Baseball players—
United States—Anecdotes.   I. Title.   II. Series: Shannon, Mike.
Baseball tales.
GV873.S42   1999
796.357'0973—dc21   98-48296
                                                                CIP

Jacket design by Kim Bartko
Front jacket illustration copyright © Todd L. W. Doney
Back jacket, flap, and interior illustrations by Don Pollard

Published by Contemporary Books
A division of NTC/Contemporary Publishing Group, Inc.
4255 West Touhy Avenue, Lincolnwood (Chicago), Illinois 60646-1975 U.S.A.
Copyright © 1999 by Mike Shannon
Printed in the United States of America
International Standard Book Number: 0-8092-2771-1
99 00 01 02 03 04 QP 18 17 16 15 14 13 12 11 10 9 8 7 6 5 4 3 2 1

CONTENTS

PREFACE

The summer of '98 will always be easy for me to remember. As Mark McGwire and Sammy Sosa kept refocusing the nation's distracted attention on their Herculean assault on Roger Maris's suddenly ancient and vulnerable home-run record, I couldn't manage a single base hit. No, I'm not that bad a hitter. It's that, for the first time in almost twenty years, I didn't even get the chance to play fast-pitch softball.

The year before, I had played first base for a team full of veteran fast-pitch players called the Miami Valley Merchants. The core of the team lived in the Dayton, Ohio, area, but others lived in Hamilton, Cincinnati, and northern Kentucky. For the 1998 season we had even recruited a shortstop who was going to drive in from Pennsylvania to play with us every weekend.

It was Joe Stephenson who called me with the bad news for the 1998 season. Joe is a burly, short-haired, good ol' boy from South Carolina. We met about fifteen years ago when I was still running my own fast-pitch team. Joe had just moved to Ft. Wright, Kentucky, his wife Gretchen's hometown, and the first thing Joe wanted to do was to hook up with a fast-pitch team. I didn't waste any time either. "Are you any good?" I asked him on the phone.

"Just give me a tryout and you can decide for yourself," Joe said. It took me about five minutes to realize that Joe would be the best player on our team. He had all five tools.

I'll never forget the first time we played together. It was the first game of a doubleheader in Georgetown, Kentucky. A

Georgetown batter lofted a medium fly ball into dead center. Joe camped under it, caught it, and then dropped it. Back in the dugout, Joe announced, to himself as much as to anyone else, "That'll never happen again." He said this not as an excuse or a hope or a fear but as a simple fact. And I've never seen Joe drop another one; on the other hand, I've seen him make a lot of what ballplayers, both amateur and professional, love to call "major league plays."

The 1998 Miami Valley Merchants' season was scheduled to open the weekend of Saturday, May 16, and Sunday, May 17, in Anderson, Indiana. We were going to play in the Reeder Heating Classic. Earlier in the week I had received a couple of calls from Jeff Hershner and Brett Domescik, two of the Dayton guys who ran the team, double-checking to make sure I was going to make the trip to Anderson. I should have known something was up, but I was surprised when Joe called me Friday night and said, "You can sleep in tomorrow. We're not going to Indiana. We've only got seven guys who are ready to go, so Jeff and Brett have decided to shut the whole thing down right now."

So that was it. The Miami Valley Merchants were through for the season before it even started. All it took to dissolve the team, to wipe out the entire schedule, to cancel a summer's worth of weekend trips all over the state of Ohio (plus a couple of trips to neighboring states) were a few phone calls. It didn't seem right for such a thing to occur, for an enterprise as fun and wholesome as a competitive fast-pitch team full of serious, dedicated players to be snuffed out so easily, but the sad truth is that we didn't really have a team full of serious, dedicated players anymore.

I'm hoping, of course, that the demise of the Merchants is only temporary, that the team will be resurrected in 1999. I don't want to be party to the disbanding of another fast-pitch team. The team I'd organized and managed fizzled out, after an eight-year run, during a humiliating weekend tournament pockmarked by no-shows and fill-ins coaxed out of the stands. Three years later, I was a member of the last Hamilton Merchants squad, a team that, under a succession of different names, had been a well-known force in Ohio fast-pitch circles for more than thirty years.

The Hamilton "program," as he called it, had been run by Murel Phillips (pronounced "Merle"), a chain-smoking old fart who had been a great fast-pitch catcher in his younger days. In his managerial heyday when the game was stronger, Murel had often been unable to control his acerbic tongue, and he had practically out-Steinbrennered the owner of the New York Yankees in the way he'd mishandled players and made ruthless and sometimes underhanded roster moves. On the other hand, Murel was an excellent judge of talent and character, and when he wanted to he could charm the crudest barmaid into acting like the sweetest debutante. He often spoke in fast-pitch parables, declining to make his point directly, preferring instead to tell a long-winded story about some player or game from the past so that the listener, if he had the sense to do so, could extrapolate the point of the story and apply it to his own situation. And always, his speech was a colorful mixture of homey expressions, archaic words, malapropisms, and fast-pitch proverbs. One of his favorite expressions, meant to say we weren't going to talk a long time, was "There's no need for us to go up the hill and down the mountain," but we always did anyway.

Murel loved to gather us into a huddle for a last few words of encouragement or advice right before it was time for us to take our positions on the field. The problem with that, of course, is that once Murel got started, it was hard for him to stop. Our sweet-swinging third baseman–center fielder, Matt Wynn, loved to help him, though. When Matt had heard enough, he would thrust his arm into the middle of the huddle—the whole team following suit—and then, as Murel continued his pep talk, Matt would lead the cheer that would culminate in the upthrusting of hands and the jocular disbandment of the meeting: "Okay, everybody . . . One, two, three . . . Let's . . . WIIIIN!!!"

By the time I played for him, the years, the shriveling of the sport, and his poor health had mellowed him considerably. Still, he lived for fast-pitch—two of the tournaments we hosted were named in memory of his deceased wife, Lenora, and their deceased daughter, Tina—and I came to realize, during that last year of his life, that for him, his interminable fast-pitch telephone monologues that everyone dreaded were much more pleasure than business. He died in the fall of 1996, and the Hamilton Merchants ball club did not assemble for even one let's-see-if-we-can-keep-this-thing-together spring practice.

When Satchel Paige was asked how he felt about making his rookie debut in the white major leagues as a Cleveland Indian in 1948, he supposedly sneered, "Whoever heard of a forty-year-old rookie?" Like Satchel, when I played my first fast-pitch game I was too old to be considered a rookie. Years before I had retired from baseball in favor of coaching, but two school-teaching chums in Cincinnati, Tom Betts and Mike Hupfer, talked me into subbing on their fast-pitch team. They had both grown up in Iowa, where fast-pitch softball was and still is a big deal. Hupfer teased me just enough, asking: "Can you knock down a ground ball and make a decent throw to first?"

I didn't do very well in that first game, which we lost. Going into the game I was pretty nervous, having not played anything more athletic than Chinese checkers in a while and remembering how my college-age baseball friends and I had watched fast-pitch softball games down in Jacksonville, Florida, a decade earlier and marveled at the seeming impossibility of hitting pitches, delivered by grizzled truck drivers and construction workers a mere forty-six feet from home plate, that sped past the batters like blips on a radar screen, all the while rising sometimes from the knees to the armpits.

It shouldn't have bothered me, not hitting the ball, because I really had no intention of playing again, but it did. I stayed after to watch the next game and wound up subbing again, for a different team. I had already learned to swing a little over the ball to compensate for the pitchers' natural risers, and when I smashed a line drive past the third baseman and into left field for my first fast-pitch hit, I was hooked.

Now I'm reluctant to go back to the smaller ball and the longer bases of baseball (fast-pitch bases are thirty feet shorter)—even though I could probably compete just fine in the over-forty league, which I'm eligible for—not just because I'm older and baseball-rusty but because I don't want to abandon fast-pitch. These days too many good things are surrendered without a fight, and fast-pitch softball is a beautiful game that deserves to be preserved. (Since fast-pitch permits stealing and bunting and is centered around a real duel between pitcher and hitter, I started to say that fast-pitch is an extremely similar derivative of baseball. Actually, fast-pitch can be said to be a precursor of baseball, since in the beginning, baseball pitchers threw underhanded, and then underhanded with speed, before taking the revolutionary step of using an overhanded delivery.)

The one upside to the cancellation of the Miami Valley Merchants' season is that my weekends during the summer of 1998 were free to be devoted to the completion of *Tales from the Ballpark*. To echo the comic Yankees catcher who wanted to thank all the people who made Yogi Berra Night "necessary," this book was made "necessary" by the success of its predecessor, *Tales from the Dugout*. A lot of people had a hand in that success, none more important than the people who bought and read the book. This may be stating the obvious, but I think it is worth stating nevertheless, because book buyers and book readers are not always appreciated as they should be. In Library Science programs the "death of the book" is still a popular term-paper topic, and the prevailing wisdom, which has prevailed without being proven true for decades now, is that the book is becoming more and more obsolete, as superior (read, "cost-effective") containers of information are developed. This is not to mention the competition books and reading receive from a myriad of completely unrelated distractions and forms of entertainment. I have faith that neither the computer nor any gizmo as yet to be invented will ever eradicate the sublimely humanizing experience of book reading, no matter where future technological advances lead us. And I believe, as I'm sure you do, that the book is one of mankind's greatest achievements, an idea that deserves to be respected and defended, even more so than fast-pitch softball. So I guess what I'm saying is thank you, for being a reader and for reading *Tales from the Dugout* because it gave me the opportunity to write *Tales from the Ballpark*. And to all of you who collect as well as read baseball books, I sympathize completely if your spouse has ever said to you, "Well, if you've already read them, why do we have to keep all these books?"

Needless to say, I had a great time gathering material for *Tales from the Ballpark*. I spent a day and a half at the All Star Baseball Camp run by ex–major leaguers John Pacella and Dan Briggs at Denison University in Granville, Ohio, and I appreciate the way they stayed up half the night after a long day in the hot sun to tell me some of the most hilarious baseball stories I've ever heard. Jon Warden, one of the most personable people on the planet and a great storyteller himself, helped me meet a number of ex-ballplayers who proved to be extremely cooperative and helpful, especially two "crazy bastards" named Gary Bell and Brad Lesley. Also generous with his time was Ted Power, who told me two great stories, one funny and one tragic. In recent years Ted has been doing a lot of good work, trying to take a religiously uplifting message to underprivileged kids through sports clinics, but I sensed he felt a yearning to get back into baseball. I wasn't surprised to hear later in the summer that

Ted had taken a position as general manager for an independent minor league team in West Virginia.

I wanted to talk to one of our homegrown Cincinnati baseball heroes, Tommy Kramer, who pitches for the Colorado Sky Sox, the Rockies' Triple-A affiliate, so I took my first trip ever into the fast-pitch–rich state of Iowa to see the Sky Sox play the Iowa Cubs in Des Moines. A couple of nights before I caught up with Tommy, he broke the Sky Sox club record for saves, which had been held by the ill-fated Steve Olin, but I didn't get to see Tommy pitch in Des Moines. Despite having no advance warning of my visit because his roommate failed to pass on the message I left for him, Tommy greeted me warmly, and, as befitting the classy guy he is, did everything he could to help me with the book. I also got to ask an expert, the Sky Sox pitching coach Sonny Siebert, the question that has bedeviled all of Tommy's friends at Crosley's Sports Bar & Eatery for several years now: What does Tommy, who has proven he can pitch in the big leagues, have to do to get promoted to the Rockies? "I don't know," said Siebert. "We recommend him all the time."

Working on this book also gave me the chance to get back in touch with some old friends: high school buddy and teammate Pat McMahon, who I'm proud to say is the head baseball coach at Mississippi State University; a true original and the world's leading used-baseball-book dealer, the amazing Bobby Plapinger of Ashland, Oregon; and the Mollers (Salty, Noni, Terese, and Denny) of Chicago, who treated me in their beautiful home to what I can only describe as some of the most wonderful "southern hospitality" I've ever enjoyed.

Every book is an adventure, and doubly so when the author is required to travel. I am an intrepid traveler, but not always as organized as the IT should be. In early August I drove to Chicago to attend the 1998 National Sports Collectors Convention to interview some of the ex–major league ballplayers who were going to be there signing autographs. I couldn't find the venue, the Rosemont Convention Center, on my map, perhaps because it's difficult to read a map when you're in bumper-to-bumper traffic going 75 m.p.h.

I did the sensible thing, which every lame sitcom assures us no male has ever done: I asked for directions. I pulled off the freeway and went inside a neighborhood gas station/convenience store. "No, I'm sorry. I don't know where anything is. I just moved to America," said the clerk. Undaunted, I asked directions of a man who had his back to me as he pulled a carton of chocolate milk off a low shelf in one of the coolers. "Sure, I can tell you how to get to the Rosemont from here," the man said, "but you ought to go see my uncle, Moose Skowron. He owns a bar not far from here called 'Call Me Moose.' He's going to be at the show later today signing autographs, but he's going to be at his bar all morning."

This coincidence seemed like a sign from God, or at least something akin to the mysterious messages Ray Kinsella gets in *Shoeless Joe*. And those messages worked for Ray! Though I was anxious to meet up with friends at the convention center, I had to take this unplanned side trip that had been served up on a platter. The directions to Call Me Moose supplied by Moose's nephew, Dan, were perfect. I found Bill "Moose" Skowron sitting by himself, reading the morning paper and drinking coffee, at one of the tables in the restaurant half of the bar. Hanging on all three-and-a-half walls of the room were framed black-and-white photos of favorite ballplayers from both Chicago teams, as well as photos of Moose's Yankee teammates. With his fleshy face and balding crew cut Moose looked great, pretty much as I remember him looking on Topps baseball cards from the 1960s.

Although he wasn't sure he understood what kind of story I was looking for, Moose was willing to talk. He told me about the time Casey Stengel pinch hit for him in the World Series.

It made him so mad he threw down his bat, which bounced up and hit Casey in the shins. Another story was about a truncated tryout he had with the Cubs when he was just a kid. Moose was going to take a few cuts at the end of batting practice to show the Cubs what he could do, but when the time came for him to hit, a Cubs coach abruptly shut the bp session down. "After I got to the big leagues with the Yankees," said Moose, "I'd run into this guy now and then, and he was always trying to give me the gladhand, but I never gave that son of a bitch the time of day."

Four City of Cicero sanitation workers came in to eat, and as Moose hustled to and fro, trying to attend to their every need, one of them told me, "Moose is a great guy. We love 'im. And the food here is great too." The others nodded in agreement. Moose kept worrying about me too—"You don't want no coffee? You sure?"—so to ease his mind I ordered a beer, the first beer I'd ever ordered before noon in my life.

As they ate, the men talked about Sammy Sosa and the Cubs. Moose made a derogatory comment about the Cubs, and one of the diners said, "Moose, you shoulda played for the Cubs."

"They're a bunch of losers!" shouted Moose, making us all laugh. "I'da never made no money playing for the Cubs. Thank God, I played for the best team in baseball, the New York Yankees. Seven World Series in nine years! When's the last time the Cubs been to the Series?"

"Yeah, Moose, but the Cubs got the greatest fans in the world."

"They're all a bunch of losers too!" Moose exclaimed, and we all laughed again.

After the sanitation workers left, I tried again with Moose. I was intrigued when he mentioned that Casey Stengel had recommended dancing lessons to him when he was a rookie to improve his footwork around the first-base bag. Moose said he would have done anything to break into the Yankees' lineup, so he took lessons twice a week at the Arthur Murray Dance Studio in St. Petersburg, Florida, paid for them himself, and learned to slow-waltz, jitterbug, and dance the merengue. This might be it, I thought, but Moose couldn't remember anything funny that anybody had said when they had teased him about the lessons, and he began to lose a little patience with me when I pushed him for details. I got up to go when I realized that we'd both done our best. I didn't get a story for the book, but I'd had a great time anyway. Moose wouldn't let me pay for the beer, either. Thanks, Bill.

While in Chicago I went to Wrigley Field with NTC/Contemporary editor Rob Taylor to watch the Cubs play the Arizona Diamondbacks. It was my first time, and I found Wrigley to be as glorious as everybody says it is. We got to see Kerry Wood pitch, but he got shelled—maybe he did have a case of "tired arm," as the Cubs had suggested when they were considering holding him out of the rotation for one start. One of Kerry's less effective pitches went completely out of the ballpark, over the right-field bleachers and into the middle of Sheffield Avenue. A few moments later it came back into the park and was thrown disdainfully down upon the right-field grass, as if the entire Cubs nation were saying, "Keep this garbage on your own side of the fence!" The highlight of the game was seeing Sammy Sosa hit number forty-three, which didn't come back out of the left-field stands. A bit later Sammy hit number forty-four, a mammoth blow that soared past the upper deck and well out onto Waveland Avenue. It went considerably farther than number forty-three but also, alas, foul. No matter. Both balls gave me an indelible memory of a fine afternoon and that delicious feeling that every fan relishes of being present when some baseball history is being made. Yes, I missed fast-pitch sorely, but even without it, the summer of 1998 was a good one.

In addition to those people already mentioned, I would like to acknowledge the following persons and publications for their help in compiling some of the stories in this book: Bernie Allen, Marty Appel, Sister Mary Assumpta, CSSP, Stan Bahnsen, Dusty Baker, Rod Beaton, Michael J. Bielawa, *Bleacher Banter*, Joe Boaringer, Hal Bodley, Jim Bolger, Tom Brennaman, Tim Brown, Al Carter, Ned Colletti, Jim Crowley, Marty Cusack, Marty Demerritt, Ron Disalle, *Dodgers Dugout*, Bobby Doerr, Brett Dolan, Doc Edwards, Gary Engel, Bob "Doc" Enoch, John Erardi, John Fay, Rick Firfer, Dick Fitzgerald, *The Flatbush Faithful*, Paul Foytack, Gene "Augie" Freese (The Louisiana Legend), Bob Ganzmiller, Willis "Buster" Gardner, Lloyd Gearhart, *Giants Magazine*, Vito Giordano, George Grande, Robert Grayson, Jim Hibbs, Alice "Lefty" Hohlmayer, Phil Horn, Steve Hummer, Eddie Joost, Jeff Kingery, Bill Kintner, Kenny Kramer, Ron Kramer, Mike Krukow, Duane Kupier, Norman E. Kurland, Rocky Landsverk, John Lardner, Earl Lawson, Stephanie Leathers, Frank J. Lhotsky, Jill Lieber, Ed Lucas, Jerry Lynch, Scott MacGregor, Mark Mandernach, Rich Marazzi, Pat McEvoy, Dave Miedema, Jerry Mitchell, Steve Molay, Tom Mortenson, Mike Murphy of WSCR radio in Chicago, Mike Murphy of the San Francisco Giants, Phil Nastu, Tim Neville, T. S. O'Connell, Al Oliver, Mel Parnell, Tom Pedulla, Nancy Peters, Paul Post, Tom Puehl, *Reds Report*, Dusty Rhodes, Greg Rhodes, Ray Robinson, Billy Roebel, Dave Rosenbaum, Mark Rushing, Bobby Scott, Mark Seaman, Bobby Shantz, Jeff Shoaf, Sonny Siebert, Moose Skowron, *Sports Collectors Digest*, *Sports Illustrated*, Tracy Stallard, Larry Stone, Rick Talley, Ted Taylor, Frank Thomas, Lewis Thompson, Luis Tiant, Jeff Tilley, Tony Torchia, Tom Venditelli, Gene Walter, Brett Weber, Chris Welsh, Nick Willey, *Yankees Magazine*, Pat Zachary, Joe Zureick, and Paul Zuvella. *The Baseball Encyclopedia, Baseball by the Numbers, The Cultural Encyclopedia of Baseball, The Encyclopedia of Minor League Baseball, The Ballplayers*, and *The Dickson Baseball Dictionary* were also extremely helpful for spelling and fact-checking purposes.

Last time, I forgot three thank-yous, so I make them here: to Officer Kenny Davis, one of the very best good guys in blue; to Darrell Barrett, the visionary owner of Sports Legacy, the fantastic sports art gallery located in The Ballpark, in Arlington, Texas; and to Opie Otterstad, a beautiful person as well as an artist who paints beautifully.

Speaking of art, I feel privileged to be able to work with two artists as talented and as dedicated as Donnie Pollard and Todd Doney. Somehow, miraculously, they both surpassed in the work they did for this book the outstanding work they did for *Tales from the Dugout.*

I want to thank a number of good folks at NTC/Contemporary who are a pleasure to work with: John Nolan, Craig Bolt, Tina Chapman, Stephanie DiTullio, Maureen Musker, and the golden-voiced Husker Rob Taylor, who went above and beyond the editorial call of duty on my behalf.

Once again, special thanks must go to my parents, John and Willie Shannon; to my brothers, John and Tim; to my sisters, Susie and Laura (thanks, Sis, for setting up the book signings); to my kids (Meghann, Casey, Mickey, Babe, and Nolan Ryan); to my aunt Jane Shannon, who years ago did a kindness that helped me believe I might one day become a writer; and to Jerry Hazelbaker and Mark Schraf, who would be first-ballot inductees into the Friendship Hall of Fame if such an institution existed.

At the Cubs game I attended at Wrigley Field, Harry Caray wasn't around to lead the singing of "Take Me Out to the Ball Game" during the seventh-inning stretch. His celebrity substitute that day was Miss America. She has a pretty good voice and did a bang-up job, and I'm sure that a lot of guys in the ballpark fantasized about meeting her. But not me. I've been living for almost twenty years with an uncrowned Miss America, and when I count my many blessings, my beautiful wife, Kathy, is at the top of the list.

SISTER MARY ASSUMPTA

The Cleveland Indians have always been blessed with great fans, but "nun" more special than Sister Mary Assumpta, who has become famous for baking thousands of chocolate-chip cookies for Tribe players. A nun at the Sisters of the Holy Spirit in Cleveland since 1962, Sister Mary Assumpta has been a passionate baseball fan since she was a little girl.

"Actually I grew up in Chicago as a White Sox fan," says Sister Mary Assumpta. "My mother had a stroke six weeks after I was born and became confined to a wheelchair. I spent a lot of time with her listening to White Sox games on the radio. She taught me how to score a game and also how to pray. I owe my mother a lot.

"As for baking the cookies, that began as a thank-you. Back in the mid-eighties some of us nuns wanted to take the residents of a nursing home to an Indians game. One lady in a wheelchair didn't want to go because she thought she'd be too much trouble, so we bribed her. We promised her she'd get to meet her favorite player, outfielder Mel Hall. We didn't really know how we were going to pull that off, but after the game we made our way down to the Indians' clubhouse, and we kept knocking on the door until they opened it. Mel Hall did come out, and the lady in the wheelchair got to meet him. As a thank-you we made Mel some chocolate baseball players.

"At the end of spring training the next year we wanted to welcome the team back to town, but I said I wasn't going to make any more chocolate baseball players—they were too much trouble—so I baked some chocolate-chip cookies instead. The players seemed to really like them, and after that whenever the team would go into a slump, somebody would say, 'They need some more cookies!' and I'd start baking again."

It is estimated that since 1992 Sister Mary Assumpta has baked more than eighteen thousand cookies annually for Indians players. This kind of dedication attracted media attention to Sister Mary, and she was soon being featured in national publications and making guest appearances on national radio sports-talk shows. Assumpta also became a novelty member of the media herself, writing sports features for a Cleveland television station, conducting on-field interviews of Indians players, and working as a correspondent for *CBS This Morning* at the 1995 World Series between the Indians and the Atlanta Braves.

Sister Mary Assumpta's unique place in nun and baseball history was formally recognized when the Upper Deck Company made a baseball card of her, pictured in her official uniform—the nun's traditional black-and-white habit—of course. All of the cards were distributed at the 1997 National Sports Collectors Convention in Cleveland, Ohio, except for a small supply that Upper Deck gave to Sister Mary for her own use. Why is it not surprising to learn that for Sister Mary "her own use" means giving the cards away to anyone who makes a donation to the nursing home she works at?

STAN BAHNSEN

Stan Bahnsen pitched for six different major league teams, but most fans remember him for his exploits in 1968, when he won the American League Rookie of the Year Award as a New York Yankee for compiling a 17–12 mark with a 2.05 ERA. Bahnsen himself remembers having more fun with the Yankees (1968–1971) than with any of the other five teams he played for during his sixteen-year career in the big leagues.

"When I was with the Yankees, our manager, Ralph Houk, used to refer to the bullpen as 'The Playpen' because so many of our pitchers were both young guys and practical jokers. In 1970 four of us had a pitchers' batting contest. Fritz Peterson and I were on one team, and Mel Stottlemyre and Mike Kekich were on the other team. We kept track of the hits we got in games, and we kept score according to points. A single was worth one point, a double was worth two points, and so on. The deal was that at the end of the season the losers would have to take the winners out to dinner at a nice restaurant. The winners would be able to spend as much money as they wanted to at the dinner, and the losers wouldn't be able to say no to anything.

"Stottlemyre and Kekich won the contest, and they picked a restaurant called Trader Vic's. They went crazy and ordered four or five appetizers, a couple of bottles of wine, all kinds of exotic drinks, everything on the menu practically, but Fritz and I didn't say a word about it. They couldn't understand why we weren't complaining about them running up the bill, but they were having too good a time stuffing themselves silly to really think much about it. What they didn't know was that we had gotten ahold of Stottlemyre's American Express card and made arrangements ahead of time with the restaurant to have the whole dinner put on the card. When the bill came, we just signed for it. Of course, about a month later our little ruse was exposed. When Stottlemyre's wife in Tacoma opened up their bill from American Express and saw that huge restaurant bill, she blew her stack: 'What the hell is this?'

"We paid Stottlemyre back, but he loves to tell the story, leaving out the part about us paying him back. He says something like, 'I won the bet, but lost the money anyway because Bahnsen and Peterson are crooks!' "

"Another time we were in Milwaukee on the last day of a ten-day road trip. Mike Kekich had bought a water bed on the first day of the trip, and he'd kept it hidden from us the whole trip with help from the equipment manager because he knew that we'd do something with it if we ever got our hands on it.

"At the time, they had a promotion going on at County Stadium which involved a local auto dealership. They had built a platform on top of the scoreboard and then hoisted a new car up onto the platform. The idea was that the first player to hit for the cycle would win the car.

"Well, I paid the equipment manager ten dollars to take Kekich's water bed out of hiding and drape it—it was deflated, of course—over the car. It was really a lot of trouble to do, because he had to drag the thing up a hundred-foot catwalk inside the scoreboard. When the water bed was in place, I insisted that Kekich go do some running with me in the outfield because I knew he'd notice what we had done. He went nuts when he saw his new water bed up there. He took off to go retrieve it and he got all the way to the end of the catwalk, but he found the door there locked, so he had to go find the key to the door and climb back up.

"The funny thing about it is that Kekich got to the water bed when they were right in the middle of playing 'The Star-Spangled Banner' just before the start of the game. Elston Howard, by then one of the Yankee coaches, was the first one in the dugout to notice. He turned to the pitching coach, Jim Turner, and said, 'Is that one of your crazy pitchers up there on top of the scoreboard?' Needless to say, Ralph Houk was not amused."

Ballplayers cannot be expected to remember all the brief encounters they have with fans, despite the fact that fans remember the encounters vividly. Bahnsen was reminded of this one day in May 1998 when he was in Philadelphia signing autographs at a big card show. Thirty-seven-year-old Ron Disalle stopped by to get Bahnsen's autograph and to tell the story of his attempt to do the same thing twenty years before.

"You were with the Expos back then, and I was a college kid," Disalle told Bahnsen. "You guys were staying at the Holiday Inn on Chestnut Street. I wanted your autograph, and I hung around the lobby all day to get it. After you signed for me, you asked where the team bus was. I told you that it had already left. 'That's all right,' you said, 'I've got a rental car.'

As you started walking toward the hotel parking lot, I asked if I could have a ride to the ballpark. At first you said no, but you changed your mind and said, 'Aw, come on.'

"We got on the Schuylkill Expressway and should have gone east, but you headed west. At first I figured you knew where you were going. Then I realized you didn't, and I told you we were going in the wrong direction. You didn't believe me, but when we got out to the zoo you knew we were going the wrong way and you turned the car around. When we got to the ball-park, you went in where the fans parked. The guy at the ticket booth said, 'That'll be three dollars.'

"You said, 'I'm with the Expos.'

" 'You got any ID to prove that?' the guy said.

" 'No, not really,' you said.

" 'You got to pay three dollars, then,' the guy said.

"At that point you were pretty fed up, so you just floored it and we sped off. Before we could get completely away, though, the guy kicked the car!"

When Disalle finished telling the story, Bahnsen had to admit that he didn't remember any of it, although he said he could believe that he went the wrong way on the expressway. "I've done that more than once," he said, laughing. Bahnsen signed the cover of a program for Disalle, and then it was time for Disalle to move on. Other fans were waiting in line. As Disalle walked away, he called to Bahnsen over his shoulder, "Thanks for the autograph . . . and thanks for the ride!"

BALL FOUR, *REVISITED*

When *Ball Four* was published in 1970, it created quite a controversy. No other baseball book had ever been so candid (and funny) about so many previously taboo subjects, and the book made a lot of money as well as a lot of enemies for author Jim Bouton.

Although the book received some objective praise from the press, Bouton was generally vilified by the baseball establishment and the players' fraternity. Without even having read the book, many of the latter called Bouton names like "backstabbing traitor," and they subsequently treated him like a social leper, all because Bouton broke the First Commandment of Baseball, which used to be routinely posted in professional baseball locker rooms:

What you see here
What you hear here
Let it stay here
When you leave here.

As Bouton waded through all the criticism, he perceived that most of the resentment was directed at his having depicted the sexual escapades of ballplayers and at having characterized Mickey Mantle as a not-completely-perfect hero. For many New York Yankees fans and Mantle worshipers, the book's lowest blow was its revelation that it was Mantle who often led the Yankees on rooftop "beaver-shooting" patrols in the hope of seeing a shapely woman undressing in her motel room.

According to Dick Fitzgerald, a former pitcher in the Baltimore Orioles' farm system, the Yankees weren't the only major league team known to do a little beaver-shooting.

"One year in spring training down in Miami, Florida, when I was on the Orioles' forty-man roster, Miss Universe was staying at the same hotel we were in," says Fitzgerald. "She was from Colombia, South America, and of course she was very beautiful. Her sister was staying with her in the hotel as a chaperone, and a lot of guys said she was even better looking than Miss Universe. Both of these ladies were friendly, and we'd talk to them in the lobby and get our pictures taken with them.

"About eighty percent of the guys on our forty-man roster were staying at this hotel, and we had some real characters on that team, guys like Bo Belinsky and Steve Dalkowski. Belinsky was known as the biggest playboy in baseball. He was a pretty good pitcher but a Hall of Fame womanizer. He was famous for having dated actresses Ann-Margret, Connie Stevens, Tina Louise, and Mamie Van Doren. When somebody said that Miss Universe's sister was better looking than Miss Universe, Belinsky said, 'You oughta see the mother. She beats 'em both.' You might remember Dalkowski, because according to legend he threw harder than any pitcher in baseball history. He never made it because he never knew where the hell the ball was going, had almost no control whatsoever. In the low minors, Dalkowski threw a no-hitter and struck out eighteen, but he walked twenty-one and lost the game 9–8, or something like that.

"Now, all of us had our rooms on the sixth floor of this hotel. Miss Universe's room was on the fifth floor, right by the elevator, and the guys on our team drilled the door to her room full of holes. Sometimes there'd be five or six guys standing at her door trying to get a peek into the room.

"One day our manager, Paul Richards, called a team meeting in the outfield. There were two guys in suits standing on either side of Richards. When we were all seated in the grass,

Richards said, 'These two gentlemen are detectives with the Miami Police Department, and they have something to show you.' One of the detectives turned a bag upside down, and about twenty manual drills fell out of it. They had confiscated the drills from our rooms. Richards said, 'If you had anything to do with drilling holes in Miss Universe's door, or if you know anything about it, I want you to get up and stand over there by Luman'—meaning Luman Harris, who was one of Richards's coaches. Every last man, including the guys who weren't even staying at the hotel, stood up and walked over by Harris. Harris laughed like hell, but Richards's jaw dropped open, and you could see him thinking, 'There goes my whole team!'

"After Richards regained his composure and made some excuse to the detectives, he said something to the effect of 'Never mind,' and we went back to our workout. The Orioles wound up paying off the Colombian government to smooth things over; at least that was the rumor. They also called Belinsky and Dalkowski in for further questioning in a sort of internal investigation. I don't know what Belinsky said, but when they asked Dalkowski why he drilled a hole in Miss Universe's door, Steve said, 'Because I like to drill holes.' That was the best excuse he could come up with!"

BAT BOYS AND BP PITCHERS

From 1956 to 1959 Frank J. Lhotsky worked as a clubhouse boy for visiting teams at Baltimore's Memorial Stadium. Like every other clubhouse boy, Lhotsky worked long hours for low pay doing the sort of menial housework tasks he wouldn't have dreamed of doing so readily at home. Occasionally, the regular batboy for the visiting teams let Lhotsky fill in for him. While Lhotsky didn't work as a batboy very often, he did get the job for two of the most memorable games to ever take place at Memorial Stadium. On September 20, 1958, Lhotsky was the New York Yankees' batboy, as Hoyt Wilhelm pitched a 1–0 no-hitter for the Orioles. The rare starting assignment for Wilhelm was also the Hall of Fame reliever's first major league complete game. Lhotsky remembers proud Yankees players trying (to no avail) to rattle Wilhelm by derisively using his nickname, "Tilt," given to Wilhelm because of his habit of tilting his head to one side as he pitched.

Lhotsky's other memorable moment in charge of the visiting team's lumber came on June 10, 1959, and involved a batting feat that is considerably more rare than a no-hitter. The Orioles were hosting the Cleveland Indians, and with Baltimore headed for an eventual sixth-place finish, attendance at the game was very light. In his first at bat of the evening the Indians' Rocky Colavito hit a home run. A die-hard Orioles fan, Lhotsky considered it treasonous to congratulate opposing players who did well against Baltimore, so he made a point of not shaking Colavito's hand after the home run. Colavito hit home runs in his next two plate appearances, and Lhotsky still neglected to shake the slugger's hand.

Lhotsky's attitude changed, however, when Colavito came to bat for the fourth time in the game and then cracked his fourth consecutive home run. "Wow!" Lhotsky thought. "This is history in the making. The photographers from the newspapers have got to take some pictures of this." And so Lhotsky ran out to home plate, where he greeted Colavito and finally shook his hand, confident that his picture would be in all the daily newspapers the next day.

The young batboy was correct about the significance of Colavito's feat, as only two other batters (Lou Gehrig and Bobby Lowe) had accomplished it previously, but he was mistaken about the vigilance of Baltimore's newspaper photographers. None of the papers had thought it necessary to send a photographer to cover the game. When the papers got word of what had happened, they rushed photographers to Memorial Stadium to get a photo of Colavito after the game. When Lhotsky woke up the next morning, the only photos of the event he and his mother saw in the newspapers showed Colavito kissing his bat in the clubhouse after the game.

"My one and only claim to fame ended because no photographer covered the game that particular night," says Lhotsky. In view of this great disappointment, did Lhotsky regret breaking his no-congratulating-of-the-enemy resolution? "No, I don't think so. When a man hits four consecutive home runs, the least he deserves is a handshake . . . even when he does it against my Orioles."

Many behind-the-scenes jobs that are performed in support of major league baseball are not as glamorous and exciting as most fans imagine them to be. For instance, Tim Neville, who used to pitch batting practice for the Seattle Mariners, says that he was treated as if he were "a notch below a bat or a dirty towel."

"One time a Mariners player hit a vicious line drive right back at me," says Neville. "My glove was full of baseballs, so I wasn't able to stick it up and defend myself with it, and since the ball was hit too hard for me to duck, it caught me square in the right biceps. I thought it might have broken my arm, and I was afraid to look at it. The player who hit the ball didn't ask me if I was okay or express any concern for me whatsoever. He just got irritated and screamed, 'How many times do I have to tell you batting practice guys to stay behind the screen!'

"Another time, this same player, whom I won't name for obvious reasons, was taking bp against a friend of mine, a sweet old guy who had pitched professionally in his younger days. Now, my friend was almost sixty years old, but he was still able to throw pretty good batting practice. He threw a couple of batting practice fastballs that happened to tail in on this player, and when the guy swung at them and missed, he got so mad he threw his bat at my friend. The guy was convinced that my friend was throwing him sliders, trying to strike him out."

Neville became a batting practice pitcher because he loved baseball and because he thought it would be good exercise. He knew he wasn't going to get rich doing it. In fact, a parking pass and a couple of tickets to the game on the nights he worked were the only compensation he received the first two years he threw bp for the Mariners. Finally, at the start of his third season, he was told he would actually get paid for his services: $20 per game. As things turned out, with penny-pinching owner George Argyros in charge of the Mariners' purse strings, it would have been easier for Neville to have robbed a bank.

At no time during the season did anyone ever offer to pay him, so Neville kept track of the games he worked on a pocket Mariners schedule. At the end of the season the Mariners owed him $1,020. Before the last game of the season, Neville asked the Seattle clubhouse manager whom he should turn the schedule in to. The clubhouse manager said, "It doesn't matter, you won't get paid."

"What do you mean, 'I won't get paid'?" asked Neville.

"Look, Tim, I've had a request in for six months for a hundred-dollar stainless-steel bucket that we need for the trainer's room, and George won't approve the request."

"Hey, George runs a real estate empire, an airline, and a major league baseball team. He doesn't get involved in hundred-dollar decisions," said Neville.

"Trust me, you're not getting paid," repeated the clubhouse manager.

After getting the "check-is-in-the-mail" runaround for months from a succession of Mariners front-office employees, Neville filed suit in small-claims court. This probably wouldn't have done much good, but fortunately for Neville a writer for *The Seattle Times* who specialized in stories about the struggles of the little guy caught wind of Neville's predicament and wrote a column satirizing the Mariners' cheapness and ineptness on the field. "The guy wrote something like 'Neville's job was to throw watermelon-size batting practice so that Mariners sluggers could bang the ball to the far reaches of the infield,'" says Neville. "The Mariners were so embarrassed by the column that they finally paid me, but so much for your employer showing appreciation for your labor."

With the Mariners, Neville found it possible to get in trouble just for doing his job exactly as he was told to do it. "Vada Pinson, the Mariners' batting coach, was the person in charge of the batting practice pitchers," says Neville, "and his exact words to me the day I was hired were 'Throw to whoever's out there on the field who wants to hit.'

"One day I got to the Kingdome very early, and after I got dressed and walked onto the field I saw Gaylord Perry standing around talking to a couple of the young guys who worked in the clubhouse. This was two nights after Gaylord had won his three-hundredth game in the major leagues, and he was still higher than a kite about it. The three-hundredth win was not only the highlight of Gaylord's career, but it was also the biggest deal in the history of the Mariners' franchise up to that point. He was really enjoying himself, and on this day he decided that I was going to help him have some more fun.

"When Gaylord saw me, he said, 'Are you loose?'

"I said, 'No. But who am I gonna throw to, anyway?'

" 'Me,' he said.

"Now, Gaylord is a big, intimidating guy, and there was no way I was going to argue with him, especially when he was the toast of the town. So Gaylord and I played catch for a while to get me loose, and then I started throwing bp to him. The clubhouse kids were not starstruck by Gaylord Perry or anybody else, so they disappeared because they didn't want to shag Gaylord's bp. This meant that there was nobody at all to shag. There were ten dozen used baseballs in a couple of big pickle buckets out on the mound behind the protective screen. These were the balls that the extra men, the nonstarters, would hit in the first part of batting practice. I threw every one of those balls to Gaylord, who hit them all over the place. There were ten dozen baseballs scattered all over the Kingdome.

" 'That's it, Gaylord,' I said.

" 'No more balls?' he asked.

"'There's five dozen more in the dugout,' I said, 'but they're the brand-new balls we throw to the regulars, and I'm not touching 'em. If you want me to throw them, you'll have to be the one to bring 'em out here.'

"Gaylord did just that, and after we used them up, there were fifteen dozen balls scattered all over the field and the grandstands. I took a breather and then headed for a shower in the clubhouse. When Vada Pinson saw me, he said, 'You loose?'

"'I'm done,' I said.

"'What? Who you been throwing to?'

"'Gaylord Perry.'

"'You're not supposed to throw to the pitchers,' Pinson said. 'Pitchers don't hit in the American League!'

"I reminded Pinson that he'd told me to throw to anybody who wanted to hit, but he continued looking at me like I was dumber than dirt. Bill Plummer, the bullpen coach, was sitting nearby, and one of Plummer's responsibilities was keeping all the batting practice balls sorted. At this point Plummer was starting to get a mental image of what the Kingdome looked like. 'What did you throw to him?' he asked me.

"'I threw all the extra men's balls, and Gaylord had me throw the regulars' balls too.'

"As soon as I said that, Plummer's facial expression dropped in disgust. He said, 'Aw, shit!' and took off down the hallway that led out to the field. I took a quick shower and beat it, while Pinson and Plummer were walking all over the Kingdome, picking up fifteen dozen baseballs. Even though they never said anything more about it to me, I turned their displeasure to my advantage. The next night I told Perry, 'I caught a lot of grief last night for throwing you bp. You owe me.' So I got him to sign a bunch of stuff that I gave to my nephews."

BATS

Baseball bats. Hitters fuss over them, collectors treasure them, poets and artists treat them with the reverence due a sacred totem. Along with gloves and baseballs themselves, bats are the objects that define baseball and make possible the eternal duel between the pitcher and the hitter, which is the essence of the game. The baseball bat has always had a single, obvious, and glorious purpose . . . until recently, when, in a dismal, dastardly sign of the times, it has become the weapon of choice of drug dealers.

While working in the Albert Einstein Medical Trauma Program in Philadelphia, Pennsylvania, Anthony C. Berlet, Donald P. Talenti, and Stanton F. Carroll conducted a two-year study of intentional violent assaults and discovered a steadily increasing incidence of head injuries inflicted by baseball-bat-wielding drug dealers. Reporting their findings in the August 1992 *Journal of Trauma* in a paper titled "The Baseball Bat: A Popular Mechanism of Urban Injury," Berlet et al. explain that drug dealers are using baseball bats to assault people because bats can be carried openly and legally and are not viewed as weapons. Consequently, the police and the judicial system do not treat crimes of assault involving baseball bats as seriously as those committed with guns or knives. As the Philadelphia Police Department told the researchers, drug dealers now prefer baseball bats to guns and knives because they want "an efficient weapon that will not attract undue police attention. So instead of shooting someone and facing five years, they beat them senseless with a baseball bat, and they don't get prison time."

Criminals who compound the evils of drug abuse and assault with baseball bat abuse should be given punishment that fits their crimes. In a just world, such malefactors, in addition to receiving the typical sentences, would be barred from ever again experiencing the joys of playing or watching baseball. With one exception. They would continually have to watch videotape of the infamous beanball game of 1965 when the Giants' Willie Mays wept and cradled the bleeding head of the Dodgers' John Roseboro after the latter had been clubbed three times with the bat of Mays's teammate Juan Marichal.

BUDDY BELL

A clutch-hitting third baseman for the Indians, Rangers, and Reds, Buddy Bell was even more renowned for his outstanding fielding, which earned him six straight Gold Glove Awards while laboring for the Texas Rangers. Although he wasn't exactly a standup comedian in the clubhouse, Bell had a good sense of humor and loved to agitate teammates as much as the next guy.

"Major leaguers are very fashion conscious," says one of Bell's former Indians teammates, second baseman Duane Kuiper, "and Buddy was great at picking out something wrong with a guy's shirt or his shoes and giving him a hard time about it.

"One time Buddy and I had to give speeches at a luncheon at the Stadium Club. We both went out and bought new sports coats for the occasion. Before the luncheon we checked each other out: 'You look good, Buddy,' I said. 'Thanks. So do you,' he said.

"I spoke first, and then it was Buddy's turn. He really got into his speech and was gesturing for emphasis. I started giggling and could hardly keep from bursting out laughing. That's because Buddy had forgotten to take the tags off the sleeve of his new coat. The price tag was on there, the size and material tag, the store tag . . . it all looked like one giant wristband. Buddy kept looking at me, and he was getting a little mad, because he thought I was making fun of his speaking ability.

"When he finished and sat down and I told him to look at his sleeve, he said, 'Son of a bitch! Can we leave right now?'

"Whenever I see Buddy we still laugh about it. 'Size forty-four long!' I'll never forget it."

GARY BELL

A hard-throwing right-hander who pitched for Cleveland, Boston, the Seattle Pilots, and the Chicago White Sox, Gary "Ding Dong" Bell won 121 games and saved 51 more during a twelve-year major league career that ran from 1958 through 1969. Witty, garrulous, and fun-loving, Bell was popular wherever he played. As Jim Bouton's roommate on the Seattle Pilots, Bell is one of the stars of the first half of *Ball Four*. When Bell is traded by the Pilots to Chicago, Bouton quotes Seattle catcher Mike Hegan sadly musing: "Gary's the kind of guy who's good for a club even when he's not pitching well."

Bell, who now runs a sporting goods business in his hometown of San Antonio, Texas, recalls a funny story involving former Cleveland Indians clubhouse boy Billy Malone.

"Billy used to mess with my clothes all the time," says Bell. "I'd come in after the game, and my street shirt would be missing or my socks would be nailed to the ceiling. Crazy stuff like that.

"One day I came into the clubhouse wearing this expensive mohair suit—I looked slicker than owl shit on a sycamore branch—and I told him, 'Look, Billy, I'm taking my wife and some friends out to dinner to a fancy restaurant tonight after the game. I have to look good, so don't mess with my clothes. Please, don't touch them.'

" 'Okay,' he said.

"After the game I went over to my locker, and, sure enough, my pants were missing. 'All right! Where the hell are my pants, Billy?' I demanded.

" 'I don't know, Gary.'

"'You're lying, you bastard. Tell me where my pants are!' I said again.

"'Honestly, Gary, I didn't touch your pants.'

"I got Duke Sims, one of our catchers, to help me, and the two of us dragged Billy into the trainer's room. We picked Billy up and dunked him right into the whirlpool. We held his head under awhile and then let him up for some air.

"'Now you gonna tell me where my pants are?' I said.

"'I swear to God, I don't know,' he said.

"So we dunked him again and held his head under longer. This time when he came up he was really out of breath. I asked him again, 'Where the hell are my pants, you bastard?'

"And he said, 'Okay, okay. I'll tell you. . . . I'm wearing 'em.'"

Bell also tells a couple of stories about long-distance home runs. "The guy who gave up more monster shots than anybody else I ever saw was Bill Monbouquette. One time he was pitching at Fenway, and somebody hit one a mile over the Green Monster. Carl Yastrzemski was in left field that day. He was bent over in the ready position, hands on knees, and as that ball sailed out of the ballpark, he didn't even lift his head to watch it. Monbouquette got a little ticked off about that, so when they came into the dugout after the side was retired, he said to Yaz, 'Damn, Yastrzemski, you could at least make an effort on the ball.'

"Yaz said, 'Cripes, Monbo, what the hell do you want me to do? That was such a bomb that when it landed they had to close down the Massachusetts Turnpike.'"

"In Cleveland we pitchers always got on each other about the long home runs we'd give up," says Bell. "I remember one day when we were playing the Orioles in Baltimore, and Luis Tiant was pitching for us. Up to that time there had never been a ball hit completely out of Memorial Stadium, but Tiant threw one low and inside to Frank Robinson, and Robinson just totally crushed the ball. It went higher than the top of the upper deck as it sailed completely out of the ballpark.

"When Tiant came back to the dugout, I was sitting on the very end of the bench by myself, just looking up at where that home run had left the park. Tiant saw me and said, 'Kissa my ash, Bell, you sonuva-bitchy!'

"I said, 'What? I didn't say anything.'

"The very next day I looked up toward the upper deck where Robinson's home run had left the ballpark, and there was a flag there. The only thing it said was 'HERE.'

"I pointed toward it and said, 'What's that up there, Louie?'

"Tiant really went nuts then, cussing up a storm, and I couldn't stop laughing for five minutes."

VIDA BLUE

In 1971 Oakland A Vida Blue enjoyed one of the most spectacular seasons for a pitcher in modern baseball history. The twenty-two-year-old left-hander from Mansfield, Louisiana, went 24–8 with a 1.82 ERA and 301 strikeouts in 312 innings. Blue's startling dominance of American League batters, the high leg kick of his explosive delivery, the success of the A's in the early 1970s, and the catchy ring of his unusual name all combined to make him the most exciting and popular player for millions of baseball fans across the country. Even after arm and drug-abuse problems curtailed Blue's brilliance and turned him into a merely excellent pitcher, he remained a magic name, even among other ballplayers.

After an off year in 1977, Blue was traded from the A's to the San Francisco Giants. As often happens when star players switch teams, Blue's uniform number, 14, had already been issued, to Phil Nastu, a rookie pitcher from Bridgeport, Connecticut. Baseball players become very possessive of their uniform numbers, and it usually takes a bribe or a concession of some kind to get a player to relinquish his number; however, Giants assistant equipment manager Mike Murphy couldn't have had an easier time securing Blue's number for him. When Murphy asked Nastu how he felt about giving up number 14 to Blue, Nastu said, "Are you kidding me?! Vida Blue! I'm just a rookie. He can have my number, my shoes, my jockstrap, whatever he wants. Vida Blue is my idol. When I was in high school, I begged my mom to let me legally change my name. I wanted to be 'Vida Nastu!'"

DON POLLARD

PEDRO BORBON

Baseball fights usually involve more macho posturing than actual bloodletting, but former Cincinnati Reds reliever Pedro Borbon never understood this gentlemanly tradition. According to onetime Reds pitcher Freddie Norman, any semblance of a disagreement on the baseball diamond tended to turn Borbon into a wild man.

"You remember when we were playing the Mets in the 1973 playoffs, and Pete Rose and Buddy Harrelson got into it? Well, I was sitting out in the bullpen that day, and as soon as the fight started Pedro jumped up and headed for the action. Now, the bullpen had a door to it that the Mets kept locked, but Pedro wasn't about to wait for somebody to come unlock it. He simply knocked the door down, tore it right off the hinges. He was going crazy!

"Pedro took off running across the field like he was going for a touchdown in the Rose Bowl game. I mean he wanted to get there now! When he got to the infield he somehow got Buzz Capra, the Mets pitcher, in his clutches. He yanked a big glob of hair right off Capra's head and stuffed it in his back pocket. He was so crazy, he didn't even know what he was doing.

"When the fight was over, Pedro tried to put his cap back on, but it wouldn't fit. He was pulling down on the brim and the back of the cap at the same time, but it just wouldn't fit. Somebody noticed and said, 'Hey, Pedro, you've got on a Mets cap.' Pedro took the cap off his head, looked at it, saw it was indeed a Mets cap, started gnawing on it, and wound up biting a big hunk out of the brim. After the game our clubhouse man,

Bernie Stowe, was going through the pockets of the uniforms, getting them ready to wash, and he found Capra's hair in Pedro's pants. 'What the hell is this?' he thought."

Buzz Capra's cap wasn't the last thing Borbon bit on a ball diamond. During one 1975 contest a fight between the Reds and their bitter rivals the Pittsburgh Pirates resulted in a pile of wrestling ballplayers. In the role of peacemaker, Pirates pitcher Daryl Patterson began pulling people off the pile but made the mistake of grabbing Borbon, who promptly bit Patterson in the side. The Pirates team physician ordered Patterson to get a tetanus shot, and Pittsburgh's radio play-by-play broadcaster, Bob Prince, began referring to Borbon as "Dracula."

Borbon heard about Prince's wordplay and resented it. The next day he accosted Prince's partner, Nellie King, mistaking him for Prince, and demanded that he stop libeling him. King informed Pedro of the mix-up and figured he was off the hook, but Borbon then ordered King to take his demand to Prince. King at first indignantly refused to act as a message boy, but when Borbon told him he was starting to get angry, King thought about it for a moment and decided that yes, he could deliver a message to his partner from Pedro "Dracula" Borbon.

Norman tells another story about Borbon the animal lover. "A short time after he had come over to the Reds from the California Angels," says Norman, "Pedro decided he wanted to own a dog. He bought a beautiful Alaskan Malamute puppy.

"A few days later we went on a long road trip. We were going to be gone for something like twelve days, and Pedro's idea of taking care of the dog for that long a period of time was to spread a couple of pieces of newspaper on the kitchen floor and to put out twelve bowls of dog food. I guess he'd never heard of a kennel.

"Well, when we got back to town and Pedro opened the door to his apartment, the smell almost knocked him over. The puppy had gone to the bathroom all over the apartment, and he had chewed up every stick of furniture in the place. Pedro got this disappointed look on his face and said, 'Bad *perro*! Why you want to do this to Pedro?'

"The kicker is that all the furniture was rented, and Pedro actually had the gall to try to return it to get his deposit back!"

BOB BRENLY

Giants pitcher Mike Krukow and catcher Bob Brenly were teammates, close friends, and clubhouse comedians in San Francisco for most of the 1980s. Here's a sample of the Brenly wit, as provided by Krukow.

"A lot of guys on the Giants back then used dip, which is ground-up tobacco," says Krukow. "You don't put a big wad of it in your cheek like you do with chewing tobacco; you just put a pinch of it between your cheek and gum. The thing about dip, though, is that it is a great laxative. When you put it in your mouth, you're gonna have to go to the bathroom immediately. You can start the countdown: ten, nine, eight, seven . . . If you don't already have a newspaper or magazine in your hands, forget it. It's too late.

"One day in 1983 we were sitting around the clubhouse before the game, and one of our pitchers, Fred Breining, was pacing up and down. Breining wasn't worried about the game or his pitching but his wife. She was ready to give birth, but the baby just wouldn't come. Breining was saying, 'We've tried everything. My wife's taken castor oil, she's jumped on the trampoline, the doctor's given her a shot . . .'

"And right then, out of the corner of the locker room, comes Brenly's voice: 'GIVE HER A DIP!'"

DAN BRIGGS

A common sentiment among former major league ballplayers
is that they did not fully appreciate at the time many of the
unusual experiences they had by virtue of their big league status. Dan Briggs, who played outfield and first base (1975–82)
for the Angels, Indians, Padres, Expos, and Cubs, tells a story
that typifies this phenomenon.

"One time when I was playing for the California Angels,
Nolan Ryan got invited to the White House," says Briggs. "He
got invited because there were a lot of baseball buffs on Jimmy
Carter's staff, including Carter's press secretary, Jody Powell, who
wanted to meet him. These guys had a softball team and played
a lot of games to raise money for charity. Nolan asked me, our
second baseman Jerry Remy, and a couple of other guys to go
along with him, and we were going to go to the White House
the next time we played in Baltimore. When the time came to
go over there, Nolan was sick, but we said, 'Hey, let's go anyway.'

"We drove up to the gate, honked the horn, and when we
told 'em who we were they let us right in. Before we knew it,
we were in the middle of the White House. We weren't there
five minutes before we saw Jimmy Carter walk past us. He
opened up a cabinet and was looking for a pencil or something.
We wandered into the room where the cabinet meets, and Remy
stood at a podium and imitated Nixon talking about Watergate.
Remy had read every book that had come out on the subject,
and he really did know a lot about it. Next, we went around
looking in all the garbage cans; when one of the secretaries asked

us what we were doing, we said that we were looking for the missing tapes that exonerated Nixon. After that we got in the chow line, right in front of Carter and his wife and Vice President Walter Mondale and his wife. I'll never forget what we had to eat: chicken cordon bleu.

"After lunch, we sat in on a press conference about us giving the Panama Canal to the Panamanians. I was sitting next to Ed Bradley of *60 Minutes* fame. We were supposed to be flies on the wall, but I actually raised my hand to ask a question. I wasn't called on, but I was going to ask, 'We don't need it anyway, do we, since all our ships won't fit through there?'

"Looking back on it now, I'm amazed at how easily we gained access to the White House and how freely we were allowed to roam about. I could have sat in the President's chair if I'd wanted to. Hell, if I'da been an assassin, I could have snapped his neck in two, I was so close to him! We had a blast, but it's the sort of thing that would never happen today."

LEW BURDETTE

Pitching mostly for the Boston/Milwaukee Braves, Lew Burdette fashioned a pretty good 203–144 slate over an eighteen-year career. The hero of the 1957 World Series for winning three complete games (two by shutout), Burdette teamed with Hall of Famer Warren Spahn to give the Braves one of the best 1-2 pitching punches in baseball during the fifties and early sixties. Burdette was often accused, but never convicted, of throwing a spitball. Nevertheless, at least one opponent, third baseman Gene Freese, says he knew exactly how Burdette was able to load up without being detected.

"It was not well known, but Burdette was slightly gap-toothed," says Freese. "When he went into his windup, he would bring his hands together and raise them in front of his face. Then he'd spit on his index finger . . . pssst! . . . right between his teeth. He'd barely get his finger wet, but he only needed a tiny bit of spit to make the ball dive like you wouldn't believe. That's how he did it. They could never catch him, because when the ump called for the ball he'd throw it in the dirt, and then Del Crandall would rub it in the dirt some more before giving it to the umpire.

"Burdette had the best spitball anybody ever threw, but I could hit the hell out of him. I hit good against all the cheaters. It was the no-name guys who got me out."

HARRY CARAY

Few, if any, baseball broadcasters have ever been more loved by the hometown fans than Harry Caray was loved by fans of the Chicago Cubs. In his sixteen-year stint with the Cubs, the boisterous, excitable Caray became synonymous with the team itself. He broadcast as if he were merely a fan with a microphone . . . and a beer. "I'm a Cub fan, I'm a Bud man," Caray would say. With his oversize black eyeglass frames and raspy voice, Caray was as recognizable and twice as popular as any Chicago player. Caray was known for many things, but above all for the inimitable way he led the singing of "Take Me Out to the Ball Game" during the seventh-inning stretch of every game at Wrigley Field. His unquestionably partisan rendition ("For it's root, root, root for the Cubbies"), coupled with his irresistable cajoling to join in became his trademark.

His seventh-inning interlude became so integral to Cubs baseball that when Caray passed away in February 1998, plans were made for a host of celebrities to serve as singing subs for Harry during each game of the 1998 season.

Caray's death was followed by numerous well-deserved tributes, and everybody who was anybody in Chicago seemed to have a story to share that illustrated some facet of Harry's lovable personality. Harry was indeed lovable, and he did truly love every minute that he ever spent in a ballpark, but Chicago sports radio broadcaster Mike Murphy tells a story that shows that Harry, like the rest of us, had his moments.

"One day in 1985 the Cubs were playing at Wrigley in July or August," says Murphy. "It was the hottest day I can ever remember experiencing at a ball game—it was just brutally hot—and the game went fifteen or sixteen innings. As you may know, in a game that goes that long, everybody stands up in the fourteenth inning for a second seventh-inning stretch.

"After the game ended, I headed over to a restaurant called Kelly Mondelli's, which was a hot spot with sports people at the time. I had just gotten to the front door when a big limo pulled up to the curb. And who climbs out of the limo but Harry.

"I had never met the man in my life, but like everybody in Chicago I felt as if I knew him. I held the door open for him, and as he entered the restaurant I said, 'Hey, Harry, how you doing?'

"'I need a beer, kid,' he growled. 'One hundred and twenty degrees out there today, and I had to sing that f**king song twice!'"

Cubs fans weren't the only ones who loved Harry. Before Caray became synonymous with the Cubs, he broadcast for the St. Louis Cardinals, and their fans, too, were devoted to him.

Ned Colletti, assistant general manager for the San Francisco Giants and formerly the public relations director for the Chicago Cubs, tells the following story about Caray's St. Louis days.

"Sometime in the late sixties, Harry was hit by a car, and he broke both legs. It happened late in the year, November I think it was, and Harry went down to St. Petersburg, Florida, where the Cardinals trained in the spring, to convalesce.

"Now, Harry had never missed a game before in his broadcasting career, and all winter long in St. Louis everybody kept wondering, 'Is Harry going to be healthy enough to broadcast the Cardinals games in the new season?' It was a big, big story in St. Louis.

"When opening day in St. Louis finally arrived, the ballpark was packed. There was a microphone out on the pitcher's mound, and the crowd went wild when Harry came out of the Cardinals' dugout on crutches and slowly walked out to the mound. Leaning on his crutches, Harry announced the starting lineups for both teams. Then he started walking slowly back to the dugout. When he got about halfway back, he threw one of the crutches off to the side and kept on going. The crowd went crazy when he did it. He walked another ten steps with the remaining crutch, then tossed that one aside too, and kept on going, waving to the crowd with both hands as he went. The crowd really went crazy then.

"In the dugout, Bob Gibson wanted to know what was going on, and he said, 'Harry, I saw you down in St. Petersburg a couple of days ago, and you didn't have any crutches. What was that all about just now?'

"Harry's reply was 'Bob, that was show business.'"

ROBERTO CLEMENTE

For much of his playing career, the Pittsburgh Pirates' Roberto Clemente was depicted by some in the baseball media as being a surly, hot-dogging hypochondriac. While the Pirates' right fielder surely had his faults, there was another side to the story. Sensitive by nature and fiercely proud of his Puerto Rican heritage, Clemente felt that most of his critics were racially prejudiced against him and that because of their bias he didn't receive the acclaim he deserved. Whatever the reason for it may have been, nationwide appreciation of Clemente's talents did not come until late in his career, when his domination (both offensively and defensively) of the 1971 World Series erased any doubts about his greatness as a player. Similarly, it took another sensational event, this time a tragedy, to reveal the true tenure of the man's character. On New Year's Eve of 1972, while attempting to lead a mission of mercy to take food and medical supplies to victims of an earthquake in Nicaragua, Clemente died in a plane crash off the coast of Puerto Rico. The following year baseball waived its five-year waiting period for entry into the Hall of Fame, and Clemente was inducted.

Bob "Doc" Enoch, a Pirates bullpen catcher in the late fifties, was a friend of Clemente's and remembers things that contradict Clemente's negative media image.

"Yes, I know that Clemente had a reputation for being a hypochondriac, but I didn't see it. Bobby did have a lot of injuries, but he usually played with them. I remember one time Danny Murtaugh walked by while Clemente was on the trainer's table getting rubbed down and said, 'Bobby, you sit this one out.' And Clemente said, 'No, Skip, I play.'

"Bobby wasn't a hot dog, either. He just played the game hard. He ran hard, he slid hard, he threw hard, all the time, even in practice. Bill Virdon said, 'He practices the same way he plays.' He had that great arm, but I really don't understand how it held up, because when we'd take infield he'd throw like the game depended on it. He had a lot of mannerisms too, and people particularly remember the way he'd rotate his neck before he got into the batter's box, but he was just trying to get loosened up. He wasn't showboating.

"Bobby cared about other people, too. One day when I was no longer with the Pirates as a bullpen catcher, I went down to the visiting clubhouse at Crosley Field when the Pirates were in Cincinnati to play the Reds on a getaway day. Bobby was sitting at his locker, and I went over to see him. As we were talking I was moving my neck around, so he asked me what was the matter. I told him that my neck hurt because of an old baseball injury. In a 1958 spring training intrasquad game I had broken my neck, cracked the third cervical vertebra, when I had a collision with another player trying to catch a pop-up.

"Bobby told me to go take a shower with the water as hot as I could stand it. I did that, and when I came out of the shower beet red all over, he had me lie on the trainer's table for a massage. With his very strong hands he kneaded the muscles in my neck and back, and it felt wonderful. After the massage he told me to stand up in front of him with my back to him. He took two towels, wrapped them together into a cylindrical shape, placed them along my spine, and grabbed me in a bear hug. Then, in something similar to the Heimlich maneuver, he bent backward, pulling me toward him, lifted me off the ground, and sort of bounced me up and down for a moment. As he did, I heard a sound like a xylophone, and I felt my spine go into perfect alignment. He put me down and said, 'You'll feel better tomorrow.' Heck, I already felt better. But the thing that really impressed me was that the next night I got a call from the visitors' clubhouse in St. Louis. It was Bobby, and he wanted to know if my back was better. That was the act of a compassionate man, and I didn't need the plane crash that ended his life to know that about Bobby."

COLLECTING

On September 20, 1996, the New York auction house of Christie's East sold a baseball card of Honus Wagner for $640,500. This staggering sum is the highest price ever fetched by a single baseball card, but it did not come as a shock to veteran baseball card hobbyists who know the history and lore of the Wagner card.

The story of this most famous of baseball cards began back in 1909 when the American Tobacco Company began producing baseball cards (sized 1½ by 2½ inches) to insert as a premium in packs of their Sweet Caporal, Sovereign, and Piedmont brands of cigarettes. American Tobacco naturally wanted to include the Pittsburgh Pirates' great shortstop in the set of cards (known today in the hobby as the T206 set), and so the company contacted John Gruber, a sportswriter and the official Pirates scorekeeper, and offered him $10 to secure Wagner's written permission for the use of his likeness on the cards. Gruber wrote to Wagner about the request, but Wagner bluntly declined without stating the reason for his objection to being pictured on the cards. (Wagner also generously sent Gruber a check for $10 so that his friend would not be denied the fee offered him by American Tobacco.) Although Wagner, who smoked cigars and enjoyed chewing tobacco, did not have an aversion to tobacco per se, he may have shunned cigarettes since many in the baseball hierarchy of the era disdained cigarette smoking as a nasty, unhealthful habit. Decades later, Wagner's granddaughter stated that the reason her grandfather objected to being pictured on the cards was that he didn't want little kids buying cigarettes in an effort to obtain his baseball card. It is this story that took hold and added to the legend of the card.

Before American Tobacco could respond to Wagner's refusal by pulling his card out of production, the company printed and gave away a small, unknown number of the cards. This instant scarcity became more pronounced as time went by, and the card's scarcity and fame, the popularity of the T206 set, and Wagner's greatness all combined to make the T206 Wagner the most valuable of all baseball cards.

It is estimated that close to forty T206 Wagner cards exist. The card seldom comes on the market, and whenever it does it generates intense interest, even when the particular card is in poor condition. The T206 Wagner that Christie's auctioned in 1996 is in near mint-mint condition, making it the finest specimen known to exist. Being one of two cards with "Piedmont" printed on its back instead of the typical "Sweet Caporal" makes the card an even more rare variation.

According to *Sports Collectors Digest*, the Christie's Wagner was bought in 1987 by noted collector and dealer Bill Mastro for a mere $25,000. A year later Mastro sold it for $110,000. In 1991 the card was purchased at auction for $451,000 by hockey star Wayne Gretzky and Bruce McNall, who owned the NHL's Los Angeles Kings at the time. When McNall encountered serious legal and financial problems he sold his half of the card to Gretzky, who in turn sold the card for a reported $500,000 in 1995 to Wal-Mart for a promotional giveaway. A Florida postal worker named Patricia Gibbs won the card and consigned it to Christie's.

Bidding at Christie's on the most coveted card in the hobby started at $200,000. It took less than a minute for the price to climb to half a million dollars. Even at that lofty level more than half a dozen bidders were still in the running, including three corporations by absentee bid and Mr. Mastro, who was trying to reacquire the card. At $550,000 all but three bidders had dropped out. Richard Gelman, another well-known hobby figure, boosted the ante to $560,000, Mastro raised it another $10,000, and then a final bump up to $580,000 concluded the bidding and won the cherished card for Michael Gidwitz, a Chicago investment adviser. (The final figure of $640,500 includes the "buyer's premium" that winning bidders pay as a commission to the auction house.)

Although Gidwitz had done his own bidding early in the auction, at the $500,000 mark he turned the bidding over to a friend, Rob Lifson of Robert Edward Auctions, who continued bidding as Gidwitz's agent. The least recognized collector among the bidders, Gidwitz had hoped to retain his anonymity at least for a while, but his winning bid made him an instant hobby celebrity. After the auction Lifson revealed that Gidwitz not only possessed a huge baseball memorabilia collection worth millions but also had bid unsuccessfully on the same Wagner card in a previous auction, dropping out when the bidding passed the $300,000 mark. As for Gidwitz himself, he felt as if he had picked up a bargain. How much did Gidwitz think the card was really worth? "If somebody offered me a million dollars, I guess I would sell it," he said.

A $1 million asking price for the most valuable baseball card in the world doesn't sound completely out of line, given the established sales history of the card, but the same asking price for a Cal Ripken, Jr., home run ball sounds out of touch with reality. Here's how the latter preposterous situation came about.

On September 5, 1995, Cal Ripken, Jr., played in his 2,130th consecutive game, tying Lou Gehrig's "Iron Man" record, which many fans had thought would never be challenged. Making the game even more memorable, Ripken homered over the left-field wall in the sixth inning. The home run ball bounced off one fan's hand and landed right in the empty seat next to season-ticket holder Michael Stirn, a thirty-two-year-old carpenter, who grabbed the sensational souvenir. A collector immediately offered $2,500 for the ball, but Stirn turned him down. The Orioles organized an impromptu news conference for Stirn as the game continued and arranged for Stirn and his wife to leave Camden Yards in the ninth inning with a police escort. The next day Stirn was besieged with advice, media attention, and more offers (including one of $7,500). After much soul-searching, Stirn offered the ball to Ripken through the Orioles but never received a reply.

On September 6, the night Ripken broke the record, he hit another home run. The fan who caught that home run ball traded it to Ripken for a few thousand dollars' worth of baseball memorabilia. In the opinion of many, the value of Stirn's ball went down when Ripken homered in the record-breaking game; nevertheless, when Stirn's ball was auctioned off a couple of months later (starting with a minimum bid of $9,000) by Robert Urban (who calls himself Mr. Memorabilia), it brought a surprising $48,000.

To see how this Ripken home run ball supposedly jumped in value from $48,000 to $1 million, we have to follow another home run ball, this one hit by Ripken's former teammate Eddie Murray. In 1996 Murray capped a long career by hitting his 500th home run. It was expected that Danny Jones, the fan who caught Murray's 500th home run ball, would cash in, to the tune of perhaps as much as $20,000, but the baseball-collecting hobby world was stunned when Michael Lasky announced that he was buying the ball for a cool $500,000. The purchase made a tiny bit more sense to casual observers when Lasky was identified as the owner of Psychic Friends Network and when the terms of the deal were revealed: the purchase agreement called for Lasky to pay Jones $25,000 a year for twenty years through an annuity estimated to cost $280,000. Still, the purchase was totally incomprehensible to seasoned hobbyists, for a number of reasons: (1) the fan-unfriendly Eddie Murray is not a popular player with collectors, (2) his 500th home run was merely a milestone and did not break any record, and (3) baseballs of far greater historical significance have always sold for far less money. Among the incredulous was Barry Halper, the owner of a famous $40 million collection of baseball memorabilia. "If that [Murray] ball is worth half a million, I have fifty baseballs that are worth more," he said.

One person who found the Murray ball sale perfectly reasonable was . . . you guessed it, Mr. Memorabilia, Robert Urban, who decided that the Ripken ball he had sold at auction a year earlier for $48,000 was suddenly worth $1 million. "There's a whole new market here that people don't realize—the promotional market," said Urban, trying to explain the reason for the new price tag of the Ripken ball. "It's not about which home run is worth more. In the real world, they are twenty-, thirty-thousand-dollar balls, but in the market of promotional value, they are worth millions. Look at all the [air]time Lasky has gotten."

Despite Urban's rationale, his new asking price drew nothing but derision and animosity from collecting experts and the hobby press. Urban shouldn't have needed to consult the Psychic Friends Network to predict the typical reaction, such as this one from Bill Mastro: "The reason it's headline news is because it's so absurd. It almost builds up walls for people who intend to come into our business in a legitimate way. They see it as a bunch of scam artists.

"It's real frustrating for someone who looks at this from a professional point of view. It's almost like charlatans or con men or gypsies running around making headline news that doesn't even deserve to be in the classifieds."

Anyone having even the slightest acquaintance with Japanese baseball has heard of Sadaharu Oh, the Tokyo Giants slugger who holds the world professional baseball record for lifetime home runs with 868. Not surprisingly, the most expensive Japanese baseball card is Sadaharu Oh's rookie card, which retails for about $700 in the United States, but strangely enough it is not the most valuable Japanese baseball card. That honor is reserved for a Japanese card so elusive that one has never been found. This sounds like a contradiction, but there is a logical explanation for it.

"Without a doubt the most valuable Japanese baseball card is the only card ever made of Eiji Sawamura," says Gary Engel, a dealer who specializes in Japanese baseball cards in Santa Clarita, California. "It is the Japanese equivalent of the American Honus Wagner tobacco card that sells for half a million dollars."

According to Engel, the card is the Holy Grail of Japanese baseball cards for three reasons. First, only one card was ever made of Sawamura. He died an early death, supposedly as a kamikaze pilot in World War II, and prewar card sets were few and far between to start with. As Engel says, "It's the only card of Sawamura that can possibly exist that we know of." Second, Sawamura was the greatest hero of preprofessional Japanese baseball. When he was eighteen years old, he pitched brilliantly against a team of American major league All-Stars who barnstormed through Japan in 1934. He lost one of the games 1–0 on a ninth-inning home run to Lou Gehrig, but he struck out a lot of batters in the game, including Charlie Gehringer, Babe Ruth, Gehrig, and Jimmie Foxx in succession.

"Sawamura was so outstanding that Connie Mack tried to sign him to a contract," says Engel. "In fact, Mack succeeded, but Sawamura didn't read English, so he had no idea what it was he signed. The commissioner in charge of Japanese baseball at the time said Sawamura wasn't allowed to play professionally in America, and his rejection of Mack's contract caused such a rift in Japanese-American baseball relations that no Japanese player came over to the U.S. until the 1960s."

Due to military commitments, Sawamura played only one full season in professional baseball, but that year he turned in perhaps the greatest pitching performance in Japanese baseball history, going 33–10 with a 1.38 ERA. Sawamura's death in World War II only added to his legend and status as a national hero.

As if the first two reasons weren't enough, there is a third reason the card is esteemed above all other Japanese baseball cards: the card has never actually been found. The Sawamura card is part of a set of approximately thirty black-and-white cards that are about the size and shape of bookmarks. Some of these cards are extant, and advertising that shows a picture of the Sawamura card also exists. "So we know his card existed and we know what it looks like, but there is no known example of it," says Engel. "Japanese collectors have offered as much as ten thousand dollars for the card, but one has never surfaced."

If the card is ever found, it is as likely to be found here in the United States as in Japan. That's because the Japanese don't have the same yen for collecting that we do. Most old Japanese cards were either thrown away long ago in Japan or brought back to America by U.S. military servicemen. A Sawamura card might also bring a lot more than $10,000 at auction. "There's no telling how high it would go," says Engel, "because the card has absolutely no buy-and-sell history at all. I do know this: I'd pay ten thousand dollars for the card without thinking twice about it because it's definitely the rarest Japanese baseball card we know of, as well as the only card of the biggest prewar baseball star in Japan."

Babe Ruth used the longest (36 inches) and heaviest (48 ounces) bats in major league history, but not even the Babe could have swung Vito Giordano's famous bat. Actually, Giordano can't swing it either, but he doesn't even try, because his five-and-a-half-foot-tall Babe Ruth–model Louisville Slugger is for autographs only.

Giordano, of Howell, New Jersey, was given the big bat, a composite of wood and plastic, by his wife as a fifty-fifth-birthday present in 1993, and he has been lugging the bat to card shows ever since. He has had it signed by more than two hundred players, of varying degrees of virtuosity. Hall of Famers Hank Aaron, Whitey Ford, Stan Musial, and Brooks Robinson have autographed the bat, but so have Clete Boyer, George Crowe, Phil Linz, and Willie Miranda.

Phil Linz is notable in New York Yankees folklore for being at the center of the infamous harmonica incident of 1964. In late August of that year the third-place Yanks lost four straight in Chicago. In the back of the team bus after the game, Linz, a utility player known for his sense of humor, began tooting out a barely recognizable version of "Mary Had a Little Lamb" on his new harmonica. Manager Yogi Berra, seated at the front of the bus and in a bad mood because of the losses, ordered Linz in rather crude language to knock it off. When Linz continued playing, Berra confronted him about his insubordination and a minor row ensued, which the New York press blew out of proportion. Linz's $200 fine courtesy of Berra was more than balanced by the $20,000 endorsement deal he later received from the Horner Harmonica Company. Today Linz is well aware that fans remember him chiefly for the incident, and he is happy to help perpetuate the memory—he punctuated his signature on Giordano's bat with a drawing of a little musical note!

About Miranda, a good field–no hit shortstop of the 1950s, Giordano says, "I cherish his signature more than any of the others. He was my favorite player when I was a kid. Willie was second string to Rizzuto on the Yankees, but I used to watch him take infield all the time. I loved his movements as a fielder. He died a year after I got him to sign the bat, a week before he was going to attend a Baltimore Orioles reunion."

Giordano doesn't have Mickey Mantle's signature on the bat, but the bat has been signed by Randy Gumpert, the man who gave up Mantle's first major league home run. Nor does the bat contain a Joe DiMaggio autograph. Giordano once asked if DiMaggio would sign the bat, but the promoter of the card show they were at said that Joe D does not sign bats, period (the promoter did remind Giordano that he could get a DiMaggio signature on a photo or a piece of paper for $175). Nevertheless, most players are impressed by Giordano's bat (which is no longer made by Louisville Slugger) and feel honored to add their names to it.

As a young man Giordano dreamed of playing major league baseball himself. His claim to fame as a player is that he once pitched a game in Sing-Sing prison and struck out seventeen batters—as a member of the visiting team, of course. It's his bat that has made him something of a minor baseball celebrity for now . . . and for as long as there's room on the big bat for the autograph of one more major league player.

In recent years the most amazing new phenomenon to hit the collectibles hobby has been Beanie Babies, the little bean-bag stuffed animals made officially by the Ty Company. Beanie Babies are certainly cute and cuddly, but what has most everyone excited is the fact that a secondary market for Beanie Babies has developed almost overnight. That is, when a new Beanie Baby is issued, it retails for about $5; however, once that Beanie Baby is retired from production, the price one then has to pay to obtain it from another collector or a dealer goes up substantially, often dramatically.

The main reason Beanie Baby mania spread so quickly is that Beanie Baby dealers did not have to start their own bazaar; they simply began setting up booths at the long-running baseball card shows around the country. Most baseball card dealers did not welcome the competition from Beanie Babies, and some dealers even began to fire off hysterical complaint letters to baseball card publications. The letter writers often implied that Beanie Babies were somehow not dignified enough to be sold alongside baseball cards and that Beanie Baby dealers were practically stealing from their customers when they charged high prices for retired, hard-to-find pieces.

These ridiculous and "hypocritical" accusations did nothing to slow down the charge of the Beanie Baby juggernaut. In fact, major league baseball recognized the Beanie Baby phenomenon as a great opportunity to exploit, and major league clubs began scheduling Beanie Baby giveaway days in 1997. The promotions were so successful that fifteen major league clubs scheduled Beanie Baby giveaway days during the 1998 season.

Major league baseball gave away a commemorative Beanie Baby at the 1998 All-Star Game in Colorado, generating a frenzy typical of the promotion. "It nearly caused a riot," says baseball card/Beanie Baby dealer Steve Molay of Denver. "It was crazy. My ticket to the game cost seventy dollars, face value, but the minute you walked through the turnstile people were in your face, holding up hundred-dollar bills for your Beanie Baby, a white bear with red and blue stars named 'Glory.' Stories like people paying a thousand dollars for one 'Glory' Beanie Baby spread like wildfire, but I don't know if they were true."

If disgruntled baseball card dealers, jealous of Beanie Baby sales, were hoping that the craze would suddenly crash like the hyperinflated price of a rookie card for a player who turns out to be a bust, they were extremely disappointed by what happened toward the end of the 1998 baseball season. With the introduction of Salvino's "Bamm Beanos," beanie bears with the names and uniform numbers of major league stars embroidered on them, the crossover of Beanie Babies into the baseball card hobby was complete. And already, more and more baseball card dealers have adopted the "If-you-can't-beat-'em-join-'em" attitude. As Molay says, "Most baseball card dealers are appalled by it, but they're starting to sell them."

DIZZY DEAN

If you study the life of Dizzy Dean, you'll probably come to the conclusion that all of the fables about him are true. It seems natural to refer to the big ol' good-natured country pitcher with the blazing fastball who took baseball and the country by storm in the 1930s as "the great Dizzy Dean," but Diz doubtless would think that that was being redundant. No one ever had more self-confidence or did more boasting about his athletic prowess than Dizzy Dean. Dizzy was often criticized for his excessive boasting, but his reply was "It ain't braggin' if you can back it up." And Diz did back it up, at least for a while, and especially in 1934, when he went 30–7 with a 2.66 ERA for the World Champion St. Louis Cardinals.

Eddie Joost played shortstop in the big leagues from 1936 to 1955, and he got a memorable dose of the Dean braggadocio the very first time he met the Cardinals hurler. "The first time we played the Cardinals my rookie year, Dizzy was standing behind the cage watching batting practice," says Joost. "As I walked past the cage, he said to me, 'Who are you?'

"I gave him my name, and then he said, 'Where'd you come from?'

" 'The PCL,' I said.

" 'Where?'

" 'The Pacific Coast League.'

" 'Whadya do there?' he asked.

51

" 'What do you mean?'
" 'Whadya hit?'
" '.285,' I said.
" 'Well, hell, boy, you'll never get a hit offa me!'
"That's what Dizzy said, and he meant it, too."

JIMMY DYKES

Jimmy Dykes had a forty-year career in the major leagues as a player, manager, and coach, and enjoyed every minute of it. Even as an old man, when he was a coach for the Pittsburgh Pirates, he liked to have fun, as the following story, reported by former Pirates bullpen catcher Bob Enoch, indicates.

"We were playing in Cincinnati one Sunday afternoon, when Wally Post hit a line shot out to right field," says Enoch. "Joe Christopher, our right fielder, came in on the ball and, trying to make a shoestring catch, bent the thumb on his glove hand way back. He was sure he had broken it.

"Doc Jorgensen grabbed his medical bag, and he and manager Danny Murtaugh ran out to attend to the kneeling Christopher, who was obviously in pain. When Jorgensen opened his bag, Murtaugh, who never swore, said, 'What the —— is this?!' Doc's medical bag was filled with ham-and-cheese sandwiches.

"It turned out that Joe's thumb was only sprained, but Jorgensen was really pissed about the prank. Nobody on the ball club ever admitted to doing it, but I know that Jimmy Dykes was the one who did it."

FANS

Any business that takes its customers for granted is asking for trouble, and baseball is no exception. After enduring more than a decade of seemingly never-ending feuding between millionaire owners and millionaire players about which side would get richer faster, most fans were angered and disgusted by the strike of 1994. The ensuing cancellation of the World Series was the last straw for many fans, who vowed to never attend a major league baseball game again. When attendance drastically declined for the 1995 season, baseball realized that it had a serious problem. The clubs and the players have been trying to mend fences ever since, as they publicly acknowledge an important fact of life they should have been living by all along: it's the fans who ultimately pay all of baseball's bills and salaries. Here are some stories that focus on baseball's "third estate," the fans.

If you think baseball fans weren't burning mad about the strike, consider what happened at a radio station in Northbrook, Illinois, in the fall of 1994. The story centers around "Papa Joe" Chevalier, who was the host of a syndicated sports-talk show on the One-On-One Sports Radio Network, carried by more than sixty radio stations around the country. One night in mid-October, Chevalier was complaining on the air about the absence of the baseball playoffs. A sympathetic listener came up with an interesting way to protest the strike: all the irate baseball fans in Chevalier's audience could send him baseball cards so that they could be burned at the stake like heretics. "Papa Joe" loved the idea and designated November 4 as the date for the Great American Baseball Card Burnout.

Chevalier figured that the station might receive enough cards (maybe as many as ten thousand) to fill up a big trash barrel, but he grossly underestimated the anger of those in his audience who felt like the patsies of the national pastime. The cards kept coming and coming and coming until the station had over five hundred thousand of them! In fact, the pile of cards was so huge that, ironically, the fire department refused to issue a permit to burn them. Undaunted, Chevalier found an alternate method of destroying the cards. A local company lent the station a truck that chews up tree branches, so station personnel dumped the cards into the grinder while Chevalier broadcast live from the parking lot.

As far as anyone could tell, no particularly valuable cards were sent in to be toasted . . . er, make that "devoured" . . . but that didn't negate the point that the protest clearly made. As Chevalier told *Sports Collectors Digest*, "If the owners drop dead, there would still be Major League Baseball. If the players dropped dead, there'd still be Major League Baseball. But if the fans drop dead, there's no more Major League Baseball. End of story."

Yes, many fans were hot about the strike of '94. And, while none of the players actually wanted to go on strike, did any player do or say anything to indicate he felt some personal responsibility for the disappointment the work stoppage caused the fans? The Chicago Cubs' first baseman, Mark Grace, did.

Grace was being interviewed at a Chicago Bears pro football game in early September, about a month after the strike began, when a couple came up to him and said they'd come to town to watch Northwestern University, the Bears, and the Cubs play and wanted a refund for the Cubs game they wouldn't see. Grace reached into his wallet, pulled out a $20 bill, and gave it to them.

While there is rarely an excuse for downright rudeness, it is true that major leaguers are sometimes pushed to the limits of human patience by fans who are themselves rude, greedy, and unreasonable in their insatiable demands for autographs, recognition, and other assorted favors. For baseball to truly flourish, the relationship between fans and players, like friendship, must be a two-way street. Players don't often ask fans for anything, but when they do, it is heartwarming to see the fans come through the way they have for "the original Frank Thomas," the one who played first, third, and the outfield in the major leagues from 1951 to 1966.

Unlike most major leaguers, who feel that baseball card collecting is as childish an activity as watching Saturday-morning cartoons, Frank Thomas always collected cards. Not only that, he assembled quite a collection—namely, a run of complete Topps sets from 1951 through 1991. Unfortunately, the collection was wiped out by a fire at the Thomas home in 1992, and Thomas's insurance company would not reimburse him for his losses.

A friend of Thomas's wrote about the disaster in *Sports Collectors Digest*, and baseball fans across the country took it from there, as they began flipping through their own collections to find duplicate cards they could send Thomas to replace the ones he had lost in the fire. The replacement effort was also enhanced by a couple of collectors in Northridge, California, who made an appeal over the Internet: "If we all send Frank three cards a month, we'll have his collection rebuilt in a year and a half."

While most contributors sent three or four cards each, others were especially generous. "A guy in Springfield, Missouri, sent me a 1970 starter set," says Thomas, "and another guy in Buffalo, New York, sent a complete 1980 set. And then there was the guy who sent a Mike Schmidt rookie card, which is worth about four hundred dollars. The guy sent a note along with the card: 'Frank, I remember standing in line at the Polo Grounds to get your autograph when I was a kid. You stood there, joking and laughing, and you signed for everybody, including me. Now it's my turn to help you.' I'm not an emotional guy, but I have to admit that that brought tears to my eyes."

As of July 1998, Thomas had received enough cards to replace his lost sets from 1968 through 1991, and with continued support from collectors he was working on replacing his sets from 1951 to 1967. He was appreciative of every contribution—and showed it by sending a personal thank-you letter to every contributor—but not surprised by the responsiveness of the fans. "I've known all along that there are a lot of great baseball fans out there," says Thomas. "When I was a young ballplayer, my dad gave me that old advice: 'Be nice to everybody you meet on the way up, because you're going to meet the same people on the way down.' I always tried to remember that, and I'm glad that I did." Thomas's fans are showing that they have pretty good memories too.

Colorado Rockies fans were recently exposed to a phenomenon that went out with the 1970s—streaking. The Rockies-Reds game of April 13, 1998, was interrupted when Darren Kennedy jumped out of the left-field stands and ran toward the Rockies' startled left fielder, Dante Bichette. Security guards apprehended Kennedy almost immediately and, accompanied by laughter and cheers, dragged him off the field and through a door in the left-center-field wall.

After refocusing their attention on baseball, the Rockies went on to win the game, thereby breaking an eight-game losing streak. First baseman Greg Colburn quipped afterward, "Maybe we should take up a collection to bail the guy out of jail for helping us end the losing streak." Bichette also joked about the incident with Rockies radio broadcaster Jeff Kingery. "My dad was at the ballpark tonight, celebrating his seventy-ninth birthday," said Dante. "I told him that the fans in Denver love me, but not that much. There I was wearing purple tights with a naked guy running toward me. I can just imagine what Dad must have thought."

The next day the thirty-year-old streaker pleaded no contest to disturbing the peace, trespassing, and unlawful public indecency. He was fined $500 and received a suspended thirty-day jail sentence. Kennedy apologized to the court and said that he thought the prank would be a good way to meet women. "I've been looking for this girl to share my world," he told the judge. "I thought it would be a good idea, what I did. I know it's kind of wild. I'm sorry."

One day Luis Gonzalez was playing outfield for the Chicago Cubs when a buzz in the crowd behind him told him that something was up. When Gonzalez turned around, he saw that a fan—fully clothed, by the way—had jumped out of the bleachers and was running toward him. Gonzalez was momentarily concerned when he saw that the man was carrying a large glass jar, the lid of which he was beginning to unscrew.

As it turned out, there was no cause for alarm. A security guard was on the scene almost immediately, and he heard the man explain to Gonzalez that he was complying with the dying wish of his father, a dedicated lifelong Cubs fan, that his cremated ashes be spread over the diamond of beautiful Wrigley Field.

When the man had emptied the contents of the jar into the grass of Wrigley Field, the security guard took him by the arm and said, "Okay, fella, you're gonna have to go, but your father can stay."

Ron Kramer's favorite baseball player is his son Tom, who once tossed a one-hitter for the Cleveland Indians and who now pitches in the Colorado Rockies organization for the Triple-A Colorado Sky Sox. Long before Tom Kramer came along, Ron's favorite player was Harry Craft, who played center field for the Cincinnati Reds from 1937 to 1942. Harry Craft may not be a household name today, but here is a story about him and his biggest fan that is worth remembering.

"I'm not really sure why I was such a big Harry Craft fan," says Kramer. "He could really run and he was terrific in center field, but he didn't swing much of a bat. I do remember one time when he had gotten hot, and there was a headline in the sports page: 'Reds Climb As Craft Hits,' but that didn't happen very often. There was just something about him that I liked. He was definitely my idol. His uniform number was 23, and I adopted it as my own, wrote '#23' on everything I owned.

"In 1940 I was eight years old. In May I made my first communion, and later that same year, in October, I got confirmed. When they asked me what name I had chosen for my confirmation name, I told them 'Harry Craft.' Of course, that wasn't acceptable—as good a center fielder as he was, Harry Craft wasn't a saint—and I wound up taking my confirmation name after St. James. I was so disappointed about it that my mother told me I should write Harry Craft a letter and tell him what I'd wanted to do, so I did and then I forgot all about it.

"A couple of weeks later the mailman knocked on our door. He said, 'Ron, you've got a package here from Harry Craft!' The mailman knew who Harry Craft was, knew that he played for the Reds, and he was excited just to be delivering the package. I opened it up, and there was a major league baseball that Craft had signed and one of his gloves, which he'd also autographed across a strap on the back of the glove. It was unbelievable. You would think he might have sent a picture, but a ball and glove! Wow! I was so happy I could hardly stand it. I showed that ball and glove to everybody I knew at school and church, and after that Harry Craft couldn't do anything wrong in my eyes.

"I kept the ball on my dresser for a while, but, as kids always seem to do, I eventually played with it and messed it up. I used the glove right from the start and played with it until it completely fell apart.

"In the early sixties Craft managed the Houston ball club, and whenever they'd come into Cincinnati I'd tell myself that I ought to go down to Crosley Field to see him and tell him how much his generous gift had meant to me when I was a kid, but I never did it. Later, when my son Tommy was pitching in the minors, I thought I might run into him, but again I never did. Finally, after Tommy had made the majors, I asked him if there was any way I could find out where Harry Craft was living. Tommy said there was, and a few days later he called me with Craft's address in Conroe, Texas. I wrote him another letter. This time I thanked him, told him how much I thought of him, and tried to explain how much he did for my life back when I was a kid. I never heard back from him, and so I wasn't even sure he ever got the letter. Craft died in August of 1995, and I saw the death notice in *Baseball America*.

"A couple of years later I came home from playing in a sixty-five-and-older softball tournament and found three messages on my answering machine. All three messages were from Craft's son Tom, who lives near Dallas, Texas. When I returned his call, Tom Craft told me that he had been suffering from poor health, but that he'd finally had a chance to go through his father's papers. In doing so, he came across both my letters, which his father had saved in a file containing his most important papers and photographs from his baseball career. Tom thought I'd like to have the letters back. Tom also said that his father had told him about my original letter many years before; he said his father had always been very impressed with it and considered it one of his prized possessions.

"I'm sorry I never met Harry Craft and had the chance to thank him in person for what he did for me, but I'm very pleased to know that he treasured my letter as much as I treasured the ball and glove he sent me, and that we shared a special friendship in spirit if not in person."

FATHERS AND SONS

Baseball has long been recognized for its ability to bond together generations, and baseball lore is replete with stories about fathers and mothers handing the game down like a family heirloom to sons and daughters. Here are two stories about appreciative sons trying to give something back to their baseball-loving fathers.

In the fall of 1989 an Andover, New York, tavern owner named Pat O'Donnell planned to travel to Cooperstown, New York, with a buddy to play in a charity golf tournament. Naturally, the two friends decided that they would visit the Baseball Hall of Fame and Museum while they were in town.

For O'Donnell, the visit to the Hall of Fame would be the highlight of his life as a baseball fan, but it saddened him to think that his father, Joe, who had died in 1966, would not be around to share the experience with him. O'Donnell fondly remembered how his dad had played catcher on the semipro ball team sponsored by the company he worked for. Looking through an old family scrapbook, O'Donnell found a photo of his dad proudly wearing his Sinclair Oil Company baseball uniform. With this yellowing old photo O'Donnell devised a plan to have Big Joe O'Donnell symbolically and secretly take his place with the greatest legends in the history of the game.

Inside the Hall of Fame, O'Donnell and his friend looked about for some crevice or cranny where Pat could surreptitiously leave the treasured photo of his father, the Sinclair Oil Company catcher. They found the perfect spot in a room devoted to an exhibit about baseball during World War II. While his friend stood watch at the room's entrance and with the room otherwise deserted, O'Donnell lifted a corner of a display case on a table and slid the photo underneath. On the back of the photo O'Donnell had written the sentiments that justified this tribute to his dad:

You were never too tired to play catch.
On days off you helped build the Little League field.
You always came to watch me play.
I wish I could share this moment with you.
                         Your son,
                         Pat

The photo and the secret tribute it represented remained undisturbed for years, until remodelers began gutting the room. The photo fell to the floor and could easily have been destroyed or tossed into the garbage, but an alert cleaning lady saw it, retrieved it, and took it to curator Ted Spencer.

Spencer knew at once that the photo was an interloper. He knew that the snapshot was not Hall of Fame property. And he knew that the player depicted was nobody's hero . . . until he read the words on the back of the picture. Then Spencer understood what had happened and what the photo meant. "It was a very emotional thing from a son who thought a lot about his father," said Spencer. "Being a sobby Irishman, I fell for the story hook, line, and sinker."

Spencer felt that the photo and the son's gesture deserved preserving, but there was still one problem: no one knew who the father and son were. Eventually, *Sports Illustrated* got wind of the story. The magazine published the photo and a brief article about the anonymous father and grateful son, and the O'Donnells were promptly identified.

At first Pat O'Donnell thought he might be in trouble, but then both he and the Hall of Fame began receiving hundreds of letters from other baseball sons who were touched by the O'Donnell story. Spencer invited Pat back to Cooperstown for a meeting and explained that Big Joe's photo was going to be put back beneath the display case in the remodeled exhibit room and that, furthermore, a copy of the photo would be added to the Hall of Fame's archives, along with some of the published stories and letters connected to the incident.

It was then that Pat realized he had accomplished his original objective: catcher Joe O'Donnell was now officially enshrined as a Hall of Fame father.

Pete Rose wasn't supposed to make it to the big leagues, much less become baseball's all-time hit leader. A nay-saying succession of professional scouts, coaches, and general managers all judged that the raw, undersize park rat just didn't have the requisite physical abilities; however, during his long, joyful climb to the upper levels of baseball superstardom Rose showed that he possessed a huge heart and an iron will, as well as a great deal of previously unrecognized athletic ability. Only in retrospect does it seem obvious that Pete Rose was destined to play major league baseball.

Pete Rose, Jr., grew up basking in the spotlight that continually shone on his famous father, which is to say that he learned the rudiments of baseball, swinging fat red plastic bats at plastic balls, not in the typical suburban backyard but in major league clubhouses and on the sidelines of major league ballparks.

Given the genes Pete Junior inherited and the advantages he enjoyed, it was widely assumed that he was destined to play major league baseball. But a not-so-funny thing happened to Pete Rose, Jr., on his way to the major leagues: he got stuck in the mud of the lower minor leagues.

For nine years Rose, Jr., bounced from organization to organization, never rising above Double A and averaging a paltry .246 at bat. As if the normal hardships of minor league conditions and his own struggles weren't enough, Pete Junior also had to endure the constant abuse of loudmouthed fans, who trashed Pete Senior for having been sent to prison and mocked Pete Junior for not playing up to his father's lofty standards. Many people would have given up and started new careers, but Rose, Jr., endured. He also answered his father's critics by paying silent tribute to his great achievements: before every game he played, Pete Junior would scratch "4,256"—his father's career hit total—and "HK" for "Hit King" in the dirt near his third-base position.

Even for people as determined as Pete Rose, Jr., opportunity in professional baseball is not unlimited, and at age twenty-seven Pete Junior was running out of time. Prior to the 1997 season he was acquired as a free agent by the Cincinnati Reds. At this point his signing with the Reds had the impact of a footnote to the rest of the baseball world, but the Roses, father and son, took it as a sign that destiny was about to be fulfilled. Pete Junior spent the winter lifting weights and taking batting practice under his father's supervision. The results were immediate and dramatic, as Pete Junior tore up the Southern League for the Reds' Double-A Chattanooga team, batting .308 with 25 home runs and 98 RBI. For the first time in his career he had played like a major league prospect. Not everyone was impressed, though, particularly Reds general manager Jim Bowden.

Late in the 1997 season, with the team going nowhere, the Reds began adding some of their top minor leaguers to their roster. Asked if he was going to promote Pete Rose, Jr., Bowden said no, he wasn't. Wouldn't it be a good idea to promote

Rose, Jr., as a public relations ploy, if for no other reason? Not really, replied Bowden, because it would cost the Reds $30,000 to bring Rose up and keep him on the team for the rest of the season. *Cincinnati Enquirer* sportswriter Paul Daugherty argued that this penny-pinching rationale was not only financially short-sighted but morally untenable, as Rose had earned a promotion because of his hard work, dedication, and performance. The public agreed with Daugherty, and after receiving a flood of pro-Rose phone calls and letters the Reds announced that Rose, Jr., would join the big club on September 1.

The announcement boosted ticket sales for the September 1 game at which Rose, Jr., would make his major league debut by sixteen thousand, causing Pete Rose, Sr., attending his first game at Cinergy Field (formerly known as Riverfront Stadium) as a paying customer, to say in reference to the money Bowden was worried about spending to promote Rose, Jr., "I think the Reds made that thirty thousand back today."

When he took his position at third base to a standing ovation from the 31,920 fans in attendance, Pete Junior again scratched "4,256" and "HK" in the dirt with his spikes. And when he came to bat in the second inning against Kevin Appier of the Kansas City Royals (to another standing O), he paid another tribute to his father, standing in an exaggerated crouch and watching the first pitch from Appier all the way into the catcher's glove, just as his father had done on so many previous occasions.

Pete Junior struck out in that first at bat, but in his second try he hit a liner off first baseman Jeff King's glove that rolled out into shallow right field for the first hit of his major league career. In two more plate appearances Rose, Jr., walked and struck out again. Although the Reds lost the game 7–4, the day went down as a memorable one in Reds history. Asked if the thrill of realizing his dream was everything he thought it would be, Pete Junior said, "It was everything and more. Those nine years of bus rides, bad food, bad hotels, bad fans—it was all worth it." The father was as thrilled as the son. "He got his first big league hit," said Pete Senior. "If he never gets another one, they'll never be able to take that one away from him."

PAUL FOYTACK

An average major league pitcher, Paul Foytack did have a brief period of success when he was the mainstay of the Detroit Tigers' pitching staff from 1956 to 1959, twice winning fifteen games and twice winning fourteen. Nevertheless, he is remembered by most baseball fans for one particularly bad afternoon he spent in 1963 when he was winding up his career by toiling as a relief pitcher for the Los Angeles Angels. During the sixth inning of a July 31 game in Cleveland, Foytack set a major league record by allowing home runs to four consecutive Indians batters: Woodie Held, pitcher Pedro Ramos, Tito Francona, and Larry Brown. After the fourth consecutive home run—the first career home run by light-hitting rookie shortstop Larry Brown, no less—Angels manager Bill Rigney strolled out to the mound to consult with his presumably shell-shocked pitcher.

According to Foytack, the conversation was short.

"When Rigney reached the mound, he said, 'Well, Paul, what do you think?'

"'Gee, Bill,' I said, 'I think I'm in pretty good shape. There's nobody on base.'

"Rigney didn't think that was very funny. He growled, 'You're outta here, Foytack!' and brought in another reliever."

GENE FREESE

Playing the outfield is not easy, but it is generally easier than playing an infield position. That's why the normal procedure in professional baseball is to convert infielders to outfielders, not vice versa. Occasionally, however, an infielder has difficulty making the transition to greener pastures. Consider, for example, the experience of former Pittsburgh Pirates third baseman Gene "Augie" Freese.

"This happened when I was with the Pirates in 1956, and we were playing the Reds in Cincinnati at Crosley Field. Bobby Bragan was our manager, and he says to me, 'Can you play left field?'

"I said no, but he put me out there anyway.

"Now, Crosley Field had this steep incline in front of the wall all the way around the outfield, so that you had to run uphill to catch a ball right in front of the wall. The first fly ball hit out to me was a long one. I was playing deep to begin with, and right after I started backpedaling on it, I hit the incline and fell flat on my back. Held the guy to a double.

"About the fifth inning somebody else on the Reds hit another deep one that was over my head and toward center field. This time I tiptoed up the incline, but the next thing I knew there was no sun or sky or baseball. For a second I thought I'd gone blind. Here's what happened. Crosley Field had this giant scoreboard that jutted out in left-center field. The scorekeeper had left the door ajar, and as I was tracking that fly ball I hit the door wide open and ran completely inside the scoreboard. When my eyes adjusted, I could see the scorekeeper sitting way up

70

above me inside the scoreboard, but I didn't see no baseball. I looked out at the field and saw Bill Virdon, the center fielder, running over. 'Quail, where's it at?' I hollered. We held the guy to a triple. There's no way I coulda caught the ball since it hit way up on the scoreboard, but Bragan wasn't amused when I got back to the dugout.

"'I told you I couldn't play left field,' I said.

"'Well, maybe you'd like to take that act to Hollywood,' he said. And sure enough, he sent me out. Me, Spook Jacobs, and Luis Arroyo all got sent down to Hollywood, and they brought up Bill Mazeroski. That was the start of Maz's major league career, and it wasn't the end of mine because they brought me back up. They might not have liked my fielding, but they needed my bat to whack those pitchers!"

DON POLLARD

EDDIE GAEDEL AND
BILL VEECK

Eddie Gaedel was the midget who once batted in an actual major league game. Many people, confusing Gaedel with the diminutive character in James Thurber's famous short story "You Could Look It Up," believe that the Gaedel incident is just a myth, but it was as real as the waggish mind of St. Louis Browns owner Bill Veeck, the man who conceived and orchestrated the stunt. A promotional and publicity genius, Veeck dressed the 3'7", 65-pound Gaedel in elf slippers and a child-size Browns uniform (with the number ⅛ on the back of the shirt) and hired him to pop out of a birthday cake between games of a Browns-Tigers doubleheader on August 18, 1951, at Sportsman's Park in St. Louis. Veeck ordered the cake to celebrate the fiftieth anniversary of both the American League and the Falstaff Brewing Co., a radio sponsor of the Browns. The 18,369 fans in attendance couldn't have known it, but Gaedel and Veeck were just warming up with the birthday cake gag.

In the bottom of the first of the second game, St. Louis manager Zach Taylor sent Gaedel to the plate to pinch hit for outfielder Frank Saucier. Detroit manager Red Rolfe protested, but Veeck had thought of everything: Taylor pulled out a bona fide American League contract that Veeck had shown to umpire Ed Hurley before the game. Gaedel was allowed to bat, so to speak. As coached by Veeck, he stood motionless in a crouch, offering pitcher Bob Cain a strike zone of one and a half inches. Cain walked him on four pitches. When Jim Delsing went in to run for him, Eddie and Veeck received a standing ovation.

American League president Will Harridge was outraged with Veeck's parody and tried unsuccessfully to have Gaedel's at bat stricken from the record books. Veeck was never able to make the Browns a winner, as he had the Cleveland Indians in 1948, but he later led the 1960 Chicago White Sox to their first pennant in forty years and continued to set attendance records with his teams because of his ceaseless and innovative promotions. Veeck's antics made him a pariah with the other, stodgy owners, but baseball fans loved him, feeling a real kinship with an owner down-to-earth enough to watch a game sitting bare-chested in the bleachers. Veeck's contributions to baseball were belatedly recognized when he was selected to the Hall of Fame in 1991.

Baseball book author and former publicity director for both the New York Yankees and the Topps (baseball card) Company, Marty Appel is the man responsible for writing the inscriptions for the bronze plaques of the Hall of Fame members. When it came time to summarize Veeck's career in bronze text, Appel faced a quandary.

"The question in my mind," says Appel, "was, 'do you mention Eddie Gaedel?' It didn't seem like that single stunt was 'Hall of Fame worthy,' but it was so Veeck!

"I resolved the problem after much thought by capturing the essence of Bill and, in a subtle way, the stunt, with one final line at the bottom of the plaque:

"'A champion of the little guy.'"

LLOYD GEARHART

Outfielder Lloyd Gearhart knocked six home runs in his only season in the big leagues to help the 1947 New York Giants set a major league record (since broken) for the most home runs (221) in one season. Gearhart later scouted for the New York Mets, and he recalls that at one point he was given credit—much to his chagrin—for having more influence over the ball club than he actually had.

"Sometime in 1971 the Mets called and asked me to go watch Jim Fregosi of the California Angels. Now, Fregosi had been the Angels' shortstop and the team's best player for the last decade, but he was slowing down a bit, and the front office wanted to know how much. We needed help at second and third, and they were thinking that Fregosi could probably handle either one of those positions without any problem. So I scouted Fregosi, and I sent in my report: 'Yes, he can still play. This man can help us.' Something to that effect.

"Well, about two years later, I went to a Mets game in Cincinnati. As a scout you don't watch your own ball club very often because you're always on the road following other teams and players, and so I hadn't seen or talked to any Mets employees other than scouting personnel in a while. In December of 1971 we had traded Nolan Ryan [and three other players] to the Angels for Jim Fregosi. Fregosi didn't do much for us—and in fact we traded him to Texas halfway through the 1973 season—nor did the other three players do much for the Angels. But Ryan, he turned into a superstar almost immediately, and the New York papers were continually howling about it. I didn't understand the trade, so I asked traveling secretary Lou Niss about it. 'Why in the world did we trade Nolan Ryan?' I said.

"What are you talking about, Lloyd?" he said. "Back in New York they're blaming you for that trade."

"I couldn't believe it! I recommended Fregosi, sure, but I didn't say to get the man at all costs. And I sure as hell didn't recommend that we trade Nolan Ryan for him or for anybody else, for that matter. Ryan was still a bit wild when we had him, but you give a fella with an arm like that all the time he needs, just like the Dodgers did with Koufax. It burned me up to get blamed for that trade when I had nothing to do with it, but I guess they needed a scapegoat."

BOB GIBSON

One of baseball's greatest competitors, the St. Louis Cardinals' Bob Gibson pitched with the fury of an aggrieved Greco-Roman deity. The right-handed Gibson rode an overpowering fastball, a sharp curve, a nasty slider, and an even nastier temperament to 251 career wins and election into the Baseball Hall of Fame. Gibson never had to put on a "game face" when he went out to pitch, because he never took his game face off. He intimidated everybody, including his own teammates. Catcher Tim McCarver once called time and walked out to the mound to counsel Gibson. Before McCarver could open his mouth, Gibson snarled, "What are you doing out here on the pitcher's mound, McCarver? Get on back behind the plate. The only thing you know about pitching is that you can't hit it."

When Red Schoendienst managed the Cardinals, he didn't relish having to confront Gibson on the mound or remove him from a game, so those unpleasant responsibilities fell to pitching coach Barney Schultz, a former Cardinals knuckleballer who had pitched for St. Louis in the 1964 World Series. Gibson didn't think much more of Schultz's advice than he did McCarver's. "Barney, you were a knuckleball pitcher. I throw fastballs," he'd say.

On one of those rare occasions when Gibson didn't have very good stuff, the opposing team hit him and ran up a nice lead. Schultz called time and reluctantly trudged out toward the mound. The entire Cardinals infield could see the apprehension on the face of Schultz, who was trying to brace himself for Gibson's fiery opposition to being removed from the contest; how-

ever, as soon as Schultz got to the mound, Gibson slammed the ball into his hand, growled, "What took you so long!" and walked briskly off the field.

Although Gibson has mellowed a bit with the passing of the years, he remains an extremely proud individual, as the following Tim McCarver story indicates.

"When Steve Carlton was inducted into the Hall of Fame, I went to Cooperstown for the weekend because I had been Lefty's catcher on the Phillies. There was a dinner one night, and I was asked to come up to the front table and say something. I really didn't want to, because Steve was the guest of honor, not me, but I did it for Steve. I made a few remarks and finished with what I thought was a good conclusion: 'If Nolan Ryan will always be known for having had the best fastball, and if Sandy Koufax will always be known for having had the best curveball, and if Hoyt Wilhelm will always be known for having had the best knuckleball, then Steve Carlton will always be known for having had the best slider.'

"As I finished saying this, a man in the back of the room began elbowing his way through the crowd, saying, 'Excuse me,' 'Pardon me.' It was Bob Gibson. He came right up to my face and said with a big grin, 'You mean the best left-handed slider!'"

PUMPSIE GREEN

According to a reliable source, this next anecdote is worth a million dollars—more, with inflation taken into consideration—but it is offered here as part of this book at no extra charge.

Pumpsie Green was a light-hitting second baseman with two claims to fame. First, the Boston Red Sox were the last American League team to integrate. When Elijah Jerry Green of Oakland, California, made his major league debut with Boston in 1959, he became the first black to ever play for the Red Sox.

Second, although Green lasted only four mediocre years with the Red Sox, his was a name that made a resounding impression on America's baseball-loving youth of the sixties. There was no mystery about this, as Green's nickname was clearly more exciting than his play. "Pumpsie" connoted, if only vaguely, some darn good attributes for a ballplayer to have: drive, athleticism, energy, toughness. No matter that Green didn't actually exhibit these traits to any appreciable degree. His nickname simply had a ring that was irresistible.

In December 1962, Pumpsie was traded to the New York Mets. He spent most of 1963 with New York's Buffalo farm team, but when he was recalled to the Mets in September, he fit right in, clearly belonging on a team where the worse a man played, the more he was treated as a celebrity.

Of course, the nickname piqued a lot of curiosity. "Almost the first thing people do is ask me how I got my nickname," said Green. "I figure eight million people have asked me so far, almost half of them sportswriters. When I get out of baseball

I'm gonna write a book entitled *How I Got the Name of Pumpsie* and sell a million copies at a dollar apiece."

Green played only seventeen games for the Mets in 1963 and never graced a major league lineup again. If he ever made a million bucks later in life, it certainly wasn't through publishing the autobiography of his nickname.

So where did the name "Pumpsie" come from? This may come as a bit of a letdown to Green's fans from the sixties, but the nickname erupted not out of the white-hot fire of competition but originated with Green's mother, who called him "Pumpkin," which was later corrupted into "Pumpsie."

TONY GWYNN

Coming into the 1998 season, Tony Gwynn was the odds-on favorite to win the National League batting crown. And why not? The year before, Tony had won his fourth straight NL batting championship. Moreover, the 1997 title gave Gwynn a total of eight championships, tying him with the legendary Honus Wagner for the National League lead and leaving the immortal Ty Cobb, with his incredible twelve AL titles, as the only player left for Tony to chase.

Yes, with a lifetime batting average of .340, an unheard-of figure in the contemporary era of free swingers, Gwynn seemed poised to add a ninth Silver Bat to his trophy case at the end of the 1998 season. That's why fans across the country were shocked to open their newspapers in the middle of July and read that a career-worst 0-for-19 slump, followed shortly by a 2-for-29 hit drought, had robbed Gwynn of his confidence and reduced him to an automatic out. "Say it ain't so, Tony!" but there it was, in Tony's own words, an admission that Gwynn's head was totally screwed up. "My confidence was just shot," said Gywnn. "I know that sounds strange from a guy who's won eight batting titles and is coming up on twenty-nine hundred hits, but confidence was slipping through the windows, man. It was gone."

The slump dropped Gwynn's average down to .309 and threatened to wipe out his chances of copping the 1998 NL batting title. In the depth of his batting doldrums, when even his well-hit balls were being caught, a discouraged Gwynn said, "Right now it's a tough time, man. I'm hitting the ball good, and I keep coming back to the dugout shaking my head and thinking, 'Hey, what do I have to do?'"

Tony Gwynn is still too great a hitter to be thwarted at the plate forever, and a good series (5-for-12, 2 homers, 6 RBI) against the Reds July 17–19 helped him break out of his slump and start padding his average again.

What was the key to Tony's turnaround? Who knows? But perhaps Tony realized that what he needed to do was to take his own advice, as offered in *The Art of Hitting* by Tony Gwynn. In the chapter called "Going Bad," Gwynn says that a hitter mired in a slump needs to admit, as Tony admitted to himself when he was hitting .233 halfway through the 1988 season: "I suck. I just suck right now. I don't have to sit here and try to explain why I suck. I just know I suck."

Okay, Shakespeare it ain't. But if Tony Gwynn says that honestly coming to grips with failure is the first, pressure-reducing step toward successful slump-busting, who would want to argue with the man who comes as close as anybody alive to swinging a baseball bat as if it were a magic wand!

GIL HODGES

Gil Hodges's playing statistics, highlighted by 370 home runs, 1,274 RBI, and a career batting average of .273, may not be quite good enough to warrant a bronze plaque in Cooperstown, but no one doubts that Hodges was a Hall of Fame person. The Brooklyn Dodgers' powerful first baseman had uncommon character that revealed itself in numerous ways, but especially in the way he strove to be fair in his financial dealings with others.

Hodges originally was a catcher, but he had so much trouble catching pop-ups that the Dodgers moved him to first. Hodges's embarrassing incompetence with pop-ups continued at first base, so Gil made a deal with second baseman Jackie Robinson to pay the latter five bucks for every pop fly Robinson caught in Hodges's territory. Their unusual arrangement worked just fine until Robinson caught an infield pop-up close to first base during the 1952 World Series. As the Dodgers jogged off the field at the end of the inning, Robinson said to Hodges, "That'll be ten dollars, Gil."

"You mean five dollars, don't you?" said Hodges.

"Nope. It's ten dollars for the World Series," said Robinson.

The two of them argued some more until Hodges agreed to split the difference and pay Robinson $7.50!

In 1954 Hodges had the best year of his career. When he went into the office of Dodgers general manager Buzzie Bavasi to talk about his contract for the 1955 season, he asked for a raise to $25,000. Bavasi had already decided that Hodges deserved $27,000, but he felt he couldn't give a player more than he was asking for without appearing to be a soft touch, which would make it difficult for him to deal firmly with other players. Bavasi said, "Gil, you are a horse player, so I will put five numbers in a hat—$23,000, $24,000, $25,000, $26,000, and $27,000. The odds are three to two that you will get what you want or more."

Hodges agreed to take the gamble. He reached into the hat, and pulled out $27,000. Delighted with the outcome, the grinning Hodges nevertheless felt a twinge of guilt as he left Bavasi's office. "Sorry to do this to you, Buzzie," he said.

When the door shut behind Hodges, Bavasi had himself a good laugh. All five numbers in the hat were for $27,000!

ALICE "LEFTY" HOHLMAYER

Alice (Please, call me "Lefty") Hohlmayer pitched and played first base for the Kenosha Comets, Muskegon Lassies, Kalamazoo Lassies, and Peoria Redwings in the All American Girls Professional Baseball League (1943–54). "Lefty," who now makes autograph appearances with other former AAGPBL players at baseball card shows around the country, has two additional claims to fame: (1) she had "a boyfriend in every city in the league," and (2) she once got a hit off the legendary Satchel Paige in an exhibition game.

"In 1947 I played for the Kenosha Comets, and when the season was over I went to college at Ohio State," remembers Lefty. "That fall I got a call from Max Carey, the Hall of Famer who was president of the All American Girls League.

"'Do you want to make a hundred dollars?' he asked me.

"I said 'Sure' as fast as I could, because a hundred dollars was a lot of money in those days. When I asked Max what I had to do, he told me he wanted me to play first base in an exhibition game against the Kansas City Monarchs.

"The Monarchs were barnstorming, of course, and they had a game scheduled against Montpelier, a little town in northwest Ohio. The organizers also recruited major leaguer Bobo Newsom to pitch for this town team to give them half a chance against the Monarchs.

"The Monarchs were two and a half hours late for the game, because they went to the wrong Montpelier. Believe it or not, there's also a Montpelier in Indiana, which they went to first. The delay didn't matter, because hardly anybody left. Everybody wanted to see Satchel Paige pitch, and so there was still a big crowd for the game.

"Now, the Monarchs didn't think twice about me playing in the game. Sherwood Brewer, who played second base for the Monarchs in that game, recently said, 'We weren't shocked at the prospect of a woman playing baseball. I learned a long time ago that women can do almost anything we can do.'

"Anyway, my first time up in the game Satchel struck me out, throwing me a bunch of crazy balls. He threw me a blooper pitcher, a hesitation pitch, and a behind-the-back pitch. I was embarrassed.

"When it was my turn to bat again, I got to the plate, called time, walked halfway out to the mound, and said to Satchel, 'We're here for an exhibition. This is supposed to be for fun. You made me look bad last time. . . . Now throw me something I can hit!'

"I guess Satchel saw my point, because he started throwing me fastballs, but I popped up to short. On my third time at bat he threw me some more fastballs, and I finally hit a line drive into right field for a single.

"When Satchel got the ball back, he put his hands on his hips, turned his head toward first base, and gave me a look as if to say, 'Are you satisfied now?' Yes, I was. I felt proud of that hit then, and I'm even more proud of it today."

TRACY JONES

On Opening Day of the 1998 baseball season sportswriter Andrew Gross got pulled over by a policeman for doing fifty-five in a thirty-five-m.p.h. zone. When Gross said that he was speeding in order to get to work on time at Shea Stadium, the officer said, "In the spirit of Opening Day, I'm going to let you go."

On August 22, 1998, former Cincinnati Reds outfielder Tracy Jones wasn't so lucky. Jones, who now hosts a radio sports-talk show on the Reds' flagship station, Cincinnati's WLW, got stopped and fined for not wearing his seat belt by a Cincinnati policeman who is obviously not a baseball fan.

"The first thing you have to know is that I'm a very good driver," Jones told his radio audience that night. "I never speed or run red lights or do anything to break the law. In twenty-three years I've never had a ticket. Not a single one.

"Earlier tonight when I was on my way into work, I had just pulled onto I-71, and naturally I was listening to the Reds game on my car radio. I heard Marty Brennaman remind his listeners, as he always does, to buckle up if they were driving in their cars while listening to the game. I had forgotten to buckle my seat belt, so I reached behind me, grabbed the seat belt, and buckled it. Just as I was doing this, a cop drove past me and saw me. And can you believe that he pulled me over and gave me a ticket for not having my seat belt on?

"Now, don't get me wrong. I have always been a big supporter of the police. I have a brother who is a cop and an uncle who is a cop, but I couldn't believe this guy was actually going to write me out a ticket. I was very respectful, and I admitted that I hadn't had my seat belt on. I'm pretty sure the guy knew who I am, but that didn't make any difference to him, and neither did the fact that I put my seat belt on as soon as Marty reminded me to. I have to think that this guy is just out of the police academy—I can't believe a veteran cop would have pulled me over—either that or he has a complex about being so short. He's only about five foot two, so I guess he doesn't like guys like me who are six foot three or four.

"When I asked him how much the ticket was going to cost me, he said, 'I'm not sure. I think it's fifty-five dollars.' Where am I going to get fifty-five bucks? I guess I'll have to sell half a share of my Intel stock. But, you know, it's not the money that bothers me. It's that my perfect driving record is ruined. I was the Cal Ripken of perfect driving. I had a twenty-three-year ticketless driving streak going, but now it's over!"

RALPH KINER

Readers of *Tales from the Dugout* will remember our previous encounter with Hall of Famer Ralph Kiner, the amiable former Pirates slugger-turned-broadcaster who is famous for his malapropisms, non sequiturs, and verbal gaffes of all kinds. (During a New York Mets broadcast Kiner once said, "We'll be back with a recap after these messages.") Since Kiner is a member of the broadcasting fraternity and a member of the players' Hall of Fame, he is usually called upon at the Hall of Fame Induction Day ceremonies to introduce the winner of the Ford C. Frick Award, given for excellence in the baseball broadcasting field. *Tales from the Dugout* recounted how, in introducing the 1996 Frick Award winner, Kiner inadvertently placed the Washington Senators in the National League. During the 1997 ceremonies it looked as if Ralph were going to redeem himself, but at the very last moment he came through again with another classic Kinerism.

Jimmy Dudley, the voice of the Cleveland Indians from 1948 through 1967, was to be the recipient of the 1997 Frick Award. Because the eighty-eight-year-old Dudley was too ill to travel from his home in Tucson, Arizona, to Cooperstown, New York, to accept his award in person, someone else was at the ceremonies to stand in for him. When it was time to present the Frick Award, Kiner went to the podium, read flawlessly about Dudley's career and accomplishments, then turned to make an introduction.

"Jimmy Dudley is not able to be with us today, but here to accept his award is the Reverend Richard Dudley, Jimmy Dudley's brother."

One of the honored guests seated on the right side of the dais stood up and walked toward Kiner. When the man reached the podium, he stood close to Kiner and whispered a short message into Kiner's ear.

Kiner then turned back to the microphone and readdressed the crowd.

"Excuse me, his son!"

RAY KNIGHT

In most major league cities players and managers usually spend a day off playing golf; in Denver, Colorado, however, snow skiing is an option. April 8, 1997, was an off day for the Cincinnati Reds in Denver, and so Reds manager Ray Knight decided to go skiing with his family and pitching coach Tom Hume and his wife.

At some point during the fun Knight's daughter skied into his path. Attempting to avoid her, Knight veered off to the side, lost control, and fell six to eight feet over the side of a hill. When he landed, Knight hit his head on a small hardened mound and was briefly knocked unconscious. Doctors suspected that Knight's concussion might have been accompanied by some temporary memory loss. To test their hypothesis, one of them asked Knight the baseball equivalent of "How many fingers am I holding up?"

"Who hit 714 home runs?" asked the doctor.

"Uh . . . I don't know," answered Knight.

Under doctor's orders Knight stayed in bed another day, while batting coach Denis Menke filled in as manager for the Reds-Rockies game on April 9.

DUANE KUIPER

The immortal Babe Ruth is synonymous with the home run. By homering 714 times in 8,399 times at bat, Ruth averaged one home run every 11.7 times at bat, easily the best mark in history.

On the other end of the spectrum is Duane Kuiper (pronounced "*ky*-per") who averaged one home run every 3,379 times at bat. Kuiper's home-run average is so low because, as you may have guessed, Duane hit just the one home-run in his entire twelve-year career as a second baseman for the Cleveland Indians and San Francisco Giants. Kuiper, who now broadcasts Giants games for Fox TV, broke into the home run column playing for the Indians in his third full major league season in 1977.

"Sometimes I remember it like it was yesterday," says Kuiper, "probably because I'm reminded of it so much. We were playing at home in Cleveland's old Municipal Stadium against the Chicago White Sox, and Steve Stone was pitching. The game had a strange starting time of 8:20 because it was being broadcast as *Monday Night Baseball*. Steve Stone has always said that he wasn't properly informed about the late starting time, but I destroy that excuse by reminding him that he was loose enough to strike out Paul Dade, who led off for us in the bottom of the first inning.

"I hit it into the second or third row, about fifty feet inside the right-field foul line. It hit a seat and bounced right back to the White Sox right fielder Wayne Nordhagen. He threw it in and somebody saved it for me. The funny thing is that a great friend of mine who owned a nightclub in Cleveland didn't see this. He went out into the right-field bleachers to retrieve the ball. He offered everything for the ball: money, free drinks for a month at the club, his firstborn child . . . but nobody would cough it up. He got angry and started threatening people. Finally, he came down to the dugout to tell me he couldn't get the ball back, so I told him I already had it and he called off the dogs.

"Harry Caray, who broadcast the game for White Sox radio, later told me that he was just about to say, 'Duane Kuiper has yet to hit a home run in his major league career,' but he didn't get the words out in time.

"How did my teammates react? They were stunned, of course, but very happy for me. They all came out of the dugout and lined up to shake my hand the same way a big-time soft-ball team does. My closest friend on the team, Buddy Bell, had this huge smile on his face, as if he'd hit it himself. It's also become sort of a legend among Cleveland fans. Judging by all the people who now say they were there to witness it, you'd think the attendance that night was seventy-five thousand, but it was closer to seventy-five hundred.

"Right before my second time up in the game, I was stand-ing by the bat rack, and Bill Melton leaned over and said, 'You're not gonna use that bat again, are you?'

"'Of course,' I said. 'It's my gamer.'

"'If I were you, I'd put it away now before it gets broken. . . . You may not ever hit another one, and after you retire it'll be nice to have the bat in one piece.'

"I never dreamed I'd never hit another home run, but I guess after seeing my stroke that Melton had a pretty good idea I wouldn't. I took his advice and put the bat away, and I still have it to this day.

"Two years later we were playing the Orioles in Baltimore, when I almost hit another homer. It hit the very top of the wall, and there was some suspense for a moment as to whether it was going to bounce over the wall or bounce back in. It bounced back in, and I wound up with a triple. And guess who the pitcher was. That's right, my old buddy Steve Stone. I felt bad for him as Earl Weaver took him out of the game, but it could have been worse, if he had indeed given up two home runs to a guy who only had two home runs.

"The home run has definitely been a cross for Stoney to bear, but he's been pretty good at taking all the ribbing in stride. All those years he worked in the Cubs' broadcast booth as Harry Caray's partner, all Harry had to do to zing him was to just bring up my name. And whenever the Giants and Cubs played and our booth was next to theirs, Harry would wink at me, and I knew that Steve was about to get some grief again.

"As I said earlier, the night I hit the home run the game was being telecast as *Monday Night Baseball*. One of the announcers on that *Monday Night Baseball* crew was Al Michaels. Two or three years later Al did that Olympic hockey game during which he made that famous call, 'Do you believe in miracles?' The next time I saw him I asked him if he had first used the phrase to describe my home run. He said, 'If I didn't, I should have!' "

TOMMY LASORDA

As a minor league pitcher, Tommy Lasorda had his moments in the sun. In the low minors he once struck out twenty-five batters for the Schenectady Blue Jays in a fifteen-inning game, and his 125 career victories make him the Triple-A International League's all-time winningest pitcher. Lasorda's 0–4 major league record, compiled in brief stints with the Brooklyn Dodgers and the Kansas City Athletics, tells a different story. "Tommy had a pretty good curveball that was effective in the minors," says former Dodgers pitcher and Lasorda teammate Johnny Podres, "but he was wild with his curve, and big leaguers would lay back and wait for his fastball. It wasn't very fast."

Lasorda may not have ever pitched a major league team to victory, but as a manager he led the Los Angeles Dodgers to 1,599 wins. Only twelve managers in history won more games than that, and the accomplishment earned Lasorda a place in the Baseball Hall of Fame.

A superb motivator with a great sense of humor, Lasorda earned the title of "baseball's greatest goodwill ambassador." Claiming to "bleed Dodger Blue," Lasorda repeatedly told anyone who would listen about how great it was to be a Dodger. He loved his job so much that he gave everyone the impression that he would have done it for free.

One of Lasorda's favorite stories is about his being called upon to succeed the legendary Walter Alston as manager of the Dodgers after a long managerial apprenticeship in the minors.

"When I got promoted to the big leagues to manage the Dodgers I considered it a miracle. I said to Pee Wee Reese, who had played with me on the 1955 Brooklyn Dodgers, 'Pee Wee, if you had looked around that clubhouse and lined up every man from one to twenty-five on the chances of each of those guys someday being named to manage the Dodgers, you would have picked me number twenty-five, wouldn't you?'

"Pee Wee said, 'No, I wouldn't. I would have picked you twenty-fourth.'

"'Twenty-fourth? Who would you have picked twenty-fifth?'

"'Sandy Amoros,' said Reese. 'He couldn't speak English.'"

As fun-loving and entertaining as Lasorda was as the Dodgers manager, he knows that he would never have lasted as long as he did if he hadn't been able to produce winning teams. Tommy tells the following story to illustrate this fact of life.

"If the good Lord had decided that my lot in life was to have been a high school baseball coach, I would have told my players, 'Stay in school and then go on to college.'

"If the Lord had decided that my lot in life was to have been a college baseball coach, I would have told my players, 'Finish your education so you can become a productive member of society.'

"But I never told my Dodgers players those things, because in the major leagues you have to win! And I wanted to win in the worst way.

"Let me give you an example. One Sunday morning we were in Cincinnati. I got up and went to church, and who did I see there but the Reds manager, John McNamara. Now, I knew why I was in church, and I knew why he was in church.

"At the conclusion of Mass we walked out together, and John said, 'Wait here a minute for me, Tommy. I forgot something inside. I'll be right out.'

"Well, I sneaked in behind McNamara and I watched him. He knelt down and lit a candle, one of the candles that we Catholics light to symbolize our petitioning the Lord for a special favor.

"So when he left, I went over and blew that candle out. I knew he wasn't lighting it for a dead relative. And then I knelt down and lit a candle myself.

"That day we clobbered the Reds, beat 'em 13 to 2, and all game long I kept hollering to him from our dugout, 'It ain't gonna work, Mac. I blew it out!'

"And last year John McNamara went to Rome, and I got a card from him that said, 'Try blowing this candle out!'"

The current manager of the San Francisco Giants, Dusty Baker, played for Tommy Lasorda on the Dodgers from 1976 through 1983, and according to Baker, Lasorda was constantly either playing a joke on somebody or having a joke played on him. Lasorda also loved to catch guys breaking the rules so he could maintain an edge over them.

"One time we were staying at the Hilton in downtown Atlanta," says Baker. "It was about two or three o'clock in the morning and I was hungry, so I called room service to put in an order for some food.

" 'I want three eggs with some bacon,' I said.

" 'How you want those eggs?' the guy said.

" 'Over easy,' I told him.

" 'THREE EGGS OVER EASY AND A SLAB-O-BACON!'
I could hear this order taker shouting this to the cook in the
hotel kitchen.

" 'Give me some hash browns . . .'

" 'HASH BROWNS!'

" 'toast with lots of butter and jelly . . .'

" 'TOAST, BUTTER AND JAM!'

" 'a pot of coffee, and a glass of juice.'

" 'COFFEE AND JUICE!'

"The guy then said, 'And what room are you in, sir?'

" '1522,' I said.

" 'Dusty Baker, what are you doing up this late!' he said.

" 'Who is this?' I said.

" 'This is Tommy Lasorda, manager of the great Los Angeles Dodgers.'

" 'What are you doing in the kitchen, Tommy?' I asked him.

" 'Getting some yogurt.'

"Well, that was a laugh. First of all, Lasorda just wanted to
know who was still up. And second, there ain't no way Tommy
was gonna be in that kitchen and eat nothing but yogurt! But
Tommy was fair about it. When I convinced him that I hadn't
been out partying, that I was just hungry, he didn't fine me."

"Another time we were playing the Yankees in spring training in Fort Lauderdale," says Dusty. "I had a good friend there
named Willie who owned a T-shirt company, and I wanted to
spend some time with him. Kenny Landreaux and I played four
innings of the game and then came out, so we went off with
my friend to get something to eat. Now, the Dodgers always

flew, even during spring training, but we thought we had enough time to go out because Fort Lauderdale is not far from the airport. Well, the first four innings of the game took two hours, but the next five only took an hour. When we realized this, we got worried about missing the flight and hurried over to the airport.

"We got to the airport just in time to see the Dodger plane at the end of the runway, lifting off. 'Damn, Willie. What am I gonna do? I'm gonna be late, and Lasorda's gonna be all over my butt!'

"Willie said, 'Don't worry, Dusty. This is no problem at all.' Willie called his buddy, who just happened to own a Learjet. Within minutes we were on board that sucker and in the air. The plane was well stocked, too. The whole trip we drank Coors beer, and at the time you couldn't get it east of the Mississippi.

"We beat the Dodger plane back to Vero Beach. 'Hey, Tommy. What's up?' I said when I saw him. Oh, man, was Tommy pissed! He was sure that he had caught me good. 'How the hell did you get back? Did you leave early without permission?' he said.

"'I'm here, ain't I, and I ain't late, either,' I said.

"This time Tommy had been planning to fine me. He wanted to fine me, wanted to badly, but he really couldn't do it. I was the luckiest guy you've ever seen!"

BRAD LESLEY

Coming out of spring training in 1982, rookie pitcher Brad Lesley felt that he had earned a spot in the Cincinnati Reds' starting rotation. Pitching coach George Scherger thought otherwise, and Lesley began the season in the bullpen. The 6'7", 220-pound Lesley had a strong reaction to the decision.

"I was hot," says Lesley. "In fact, I had a bad attitude, and I decided to take it out on the hitters. Getting the hitters out was not good enough anymore. I wanted to abuse 'em. I was like a linebacker on the mound, bro. When I hit 'em, I didn't want 'em looking for my number to see who hit 'em. I wanted 'em to know it was me by the way it felt."

During Lesley's first major league appearance, a ground ball was hit to the right of first baseman Johnny Bench. As the psyched-up Lesley ran over to cover the bag, he screamed, "Give me the freaking ball, JB, GIVE ME THE BALL!" Lesley's ferocity scared Bench half to death, and after the game Bench told reporters that the pitcher had looked like a "crazed animal" running toward him. Lesley became known, instantly and for evermore, as "The Animal," and the nickname would prove to be very lucrative for him in the future.

What cemented the image of Lesley as The Animal in the public mind were his antics following a strikeout. Whenever a batter would whiff against him, Lesley, his face contorted in rage, would put an exclamation point on the strikeout by emitting a victory scream, thrusting his chest forward as he pulled his balled fists backward, and stomping around thunderously in front of the mound. It was all a tad unorthodox, but it worked.

As Lesley says, "The fans enjoyed it, and the stands came alive whenever I went into the game to pitch. My teammates loved playing defense behind me because of the quick pace I set. I didn't mess around. I got the ball and I threw it. And, best of all, the hitters starting fearing me. They thought I was a little crazy and didn't know what the heck I was gonna do next." The great Nolan Ryan even got into The Animal's act, so to speak. One day when the Reds were playing the Houston Astros, Ryan struck out a Reds batter and did an exaggerated imitation of The Animal. Ryan's big grin made it clear that he was only trying to have some fun, and Lesley took it the way it was intended. "It presented our sport in a human way and showed that ballplayers like to have fun," says Lesley. "That's what the game is all about. I was flattered that Ryan would imitate me."

Unfortunately, there were a few dissenters, chief among them Reds manager Vern Rapp, who told Lesley "to tone it down." "Shame on Vern Rapp," says Lesley. "He was wrong to tell me that, because what he was saying basically is that I was enjoying myself too much on the field. It was a win/win situation for everybody: for me, my teammates, the fans."

Nevertheless, Lesley didn't pitch much for Rapp in 1984, and after a short and forgettable stint with the Milwaukee Brewers in 1985, Lesley was finished with professional baseball in the United States. The Animal was far from dead, however.

Lesley accepted an offer from the Hankyu Braves to pitch in Japan, and he became an instant sensation. The giant, hard-throwing Lesley dominated Japanese hitters. In his first year Lesley racked up 29 saves and won the All-Star Game; in his second he went 5–3 with 19 saves. More important, the low-key Japanese were fascinated by The Animal. "They'd never seen anybody yell and scream like I did," says Lesley. The Animal was so popular, in fact, that attendance in Japan's Pacific League increased by 137 percent during Lesley's two-year career in Japanese baseball. Furthermore, unlike most American players who make no attempt to learn the Japanese language, Lesley was pretty much forced to learn to communicate in Japanese because he was single and had no wife or other family members to talk to in English. Despite occasional gaffes, such as the time he called the children of the Braves' owner "frightening" instead of "cute," Lesley made remarkable progress with the language.

Because of a contract dispute with the Braves and a good opportunity in a different field, Lesley decided to take a year off from baseball. A Japanese television network wanted him to cover National Football League games, and so they sent him to school to formally study Japanese. Lesley not only became fluent in Japanese, but he also dove into the study of the language and culture with such enthusiasm that he never returned to professional baseball.

Instead, Lesley became a major Japanese cult figure. He became an actor and starred in several movies, including *The Animal Goes to Japan*, in which he played himself. He worked as a sports commentator and hosted cooking and game shows, including one called *Challenge the Animal*. "On *Challenge the Animal* I traveled all over the country," says Brad, "from Tokyo to Sapporo, pitching against Little League teams. I was still bringing it up there around eighty miles per hour, but if the kids could hit me they won prizes." Lesley also worked as an interpreter for prominent English-speaking musicians touring Japan, such as Elton John, Eric Clapton, and Robert Cray. Lesley wound up spending ten years in Japan—"I only came back to the States twice: once to visit my mom and once for Ted Kluszewski's funeral"—and he obviously loved every minute of his stay in the Land of the Rising Sun.

Not surprisingly, Lesley's clearest memories about his days as a Japanese player involve the strange ways the Japanese have adapted baseball to their own unique culture. "They took our beautiful pastime and definitely made some changes," says Lesley. "One thing I could never get used to was the way a guy would go 4 for 4 with the game-winning RBI, and then they'd sit him down for the next game because he didn't look good in batting practice before the game.

"Another weird thing was that their answer for everything was running. Got a headache? 'MORE RUNNING!' Sore arm? 'MORE RUNNING!' Broken leg? 'MORE RUNNING!' For some reason they just believe that lots and lots of running is good for you, that it's a cure-all. One day I told 'em, 'Look, all this running is wearing me out. I'm 6'7", 270 pounds, but if you continue this running program when August rolls around I won't be able to get anybody out.' A couple of days later I was curling a little ten-pound dumbbell, and the manager shouts, 'No weight training during season! MORE RUNNING!'

"And then I'll never forget the first tie game I played in. That's right, they have ties in Japanese baseball. We were tied after twelve innings, but when I started out of the dugout to pitch the top of the thirteenth, there was the groundskeeper pulling up first base. I pointed to the scoreboard and said, 'Hey, bro, tie game. You need to leave the base there.'

" 'Time ovah,' he said. You see, all the fans ride trains to get to the games, and they have to ride trains to get home, so they put a three-hour-and-twenty-minutes time limit on the games so the fans won't miss their trains. He told me again, 'Time ovah!' And that was it: game, set, match. We went home with the game tied."

CONNIE MACK

Connie Mack (aka Cornelius McGillicuddy) is one of the most famous and revered figures in baseball history. Mack, who managed and owned the Philadelphia Athletics from 1901 to 1950, holds managerial records for most wins, losses, and games managed. Tall, thin, and somewhat gaunt, Mack never wore a baseball uniform in the dugout but was always impeccably attired in civilian clothes. He usually kept a scorecard in one hand and used it to wave his fielders into better position. He often wore a black suit and hat, and when he did he looked more like an undertaker than a baseball manager. Mack had such a strong sense of propriety that he rarely deviated from his dress code and only under the most extreme conditions. Bobby Shantz, the diminutive left-handed pitcher who won the American League MVP Award in 1952 for going 24–7, remembers one such instance. "It was in St. Louis," says Shantz. "The temperature was in the high nineties and it was extremely humid. I lost nine pounds that night pitching the ball game. The heat must have really gotten to Mr. Mack—understandably so, as he was in his eighties by then—because he took off his hat and loosened his tie. It was the only time I ever saw him out of uniform . . . that is, out of what served as his uniform."

Mack may have resembled a mortician, but he acted like a benevolent grandfather. He was taciturn, soft-spoken, pure of speech, and seldom critical of his players in front of their peers. His players loved and respected him and referred to him, as everyone else did, as "Mr. Mack." Connie was not afraid to correct his players, though, and even at the end of his career they

seldom got the best of him, as the following story by Bobby Shantz illustrates.

"This happened in 1952 or '53. We were playing in Detroit, and I was pitching. Although Mr. Mack was still in the dugout for every game, Jimmy Dykes had taken over as the manager of the A's. The first two guys in the inning got on base, so we knew the next guy, Bob Swift, would be bunting. Dykes told me to cover the third-base line, and he told our first baseman, Ferris Fain, to take anything bunted down the first-base line. Swift bunted, and the ball went between me and the third-base line. Now, I don't know why he did this, because I won eight Gold Gloves in my career, but Fain charged in and cut right in front of me to field the ball. He picked it up and threw it wild over the third baseman's head.

"After we got out of the inning and got back to the dugout, Mr. Mack went over to Ferris and, shaking his finger in front of Ferris's face, said, 'Young man, I don't ever want to see you throw a ball like that again.'

"Fain said, 'Well, what do you want me to do with it . . . stick it up my ass?'

"And Mr. Mack said, 'That would be a darn good place for it!' "

BILLY MARTIN

Nobody ever accused Billy Martin of being a politician. Billy always said exactly what he was thinking, and he often let his fists do his talking. One time Cubs pitcher Jim Brewer invaded Martin's personal space with a fastball. Martin didn't make any threats or call Brewer any names, but he did run out to the mound and slug Brewer in the face, breaking his jaw.

As a coach and manager Martin remained as feisty and direct as ever. Former Minnesota Twins second baseman Bernie Allen remembers an occasion when a Martin attempt at consolation felt more like a punch in the mouth.

"I was the guy who replaced Billy at second, and when I did the Twins made Billy a coach," says Allen. "We were playing a spring training game and a rookie made some mistake in the field. When we got back into the dugout, the manager of the team raked the kid over the coals. Then Billy walked over to him, put his arm around him, and said, 'Don't worry about it, kid. It's not your fault. . . . You don't belong up here in the first place.'"

According to the unpopular White Sox slugger Albert Belle, who should know, "It takes two days to get a bad reputation but ten years to get rid of it." Billy Martin, who had a reputation of being a hard drinker and a brawler, also knew the truth of this maxim; however, there was definitely another side to Martin not reflected by his reputation.

"Nobody ever talks about this," says Doc Enoch, a former Pirates bullpen coach, "but Billy went to Mass every day. He'd get off the team bus and say, 'Where's the nearest church?' He'd go to Mass, and then he'd head to a bar. I don't know if it made him a better person, but I do know that he was devout.

"Billy was also a very generous person. One time Billy drank a few nights with a bartender who had a lot of kids and was barely making ends meet. Every night he tipped the guy ten dollars, and on the night he left town, Billy placed a hundred-dollar bill under a napkin for the guy."

MASCOTS

Working as the mascot of a professional baseball team may have its rewards, but the job also entails a lot of hard, hot, and sweaty work. In particular, the head of the typical mascot costume can be a heavy, suffocating instrument of torture, especially during the dog days of summer. On one very hot summer day the Pittsburgh Parrot suffered heat exhaustion and passed out near second base during a game between the home-town Pirates and the New York Mets. No one came to the aid of Tom Mosser, the man inside the Parrot costume, because everybody assumed his collapse was part of his comedy routine. "I must have been out for five minutes," says Mosser. "I finally got up, stumbled across the field, and lay sprawled in an empty row of seats, in dire need of medical attention." Naturally, the fans thought the second collapse was the act's coup de grâce and cheered even more lustily than before.

Speaking of mascot heads, Billy the Marlin, the mascot of the Florida Marlins, lost his at a most inopportune moment. To kick off the Marlins' home opener of the 1997 season in a spectacular way, Billy Marlin was supposed to parachute out of an airplane, land on the mound of Pro Player Stadium in Miami, and hand ex–Marlins pitcher Charlie Hough a baseball to be used for the honorary first pitch. Actually, rather than risk the life of their mascot, the Marlins employed a stuntman for Billy, a Navy SEAL sky diver dressed as Billy. It's a good thing the Marlins did this, because not even the trained Navy SEAL was able to pull off the stunt. At about the halfway point of his seven-thousand-foot fall, the SEAL sky diver was supposed to don his five-pound Billy Marlin head, with its long pointed "bill" and large fin protruding from the back of his baseball cap, but the head was ripped from his hands and it fell to the ground in an unknown location somewhere in Dade County, where it presumably smashed into a thousand pieces.

While the Navy SEAL lost his head, he didn't lose his composure and he steered himself unobtrusively into the parking lot. Called upon to pinch hit for his pinch hitter, the real Billy the Marlin quickly dressed in a spare costume and delivered another baseball to Hough, who threw the ceremonial first pitch.

Billy the Marlin completely redeemed himself later in the season. Pro Player Stadium sold out June 13, 14, and 15 when the American League New York Yankees paid their first regular-season visit to South Florida for a historic interleague series against the National League Marlins. As part of the festivities, the Marlins and Yankees arranged for a very special person to throw out the ceremonial first pitch right before the start of the first game. The only snag was that no Marlins player was interested in being the receiving end of the pregame battery. Fortunately, Billy the Marlin agreed to catch the dignitary's toss. Still, members of the Yankee media were appalled that the Marlins' mascot was the only uniformed member of the Florida ball club willing to catch the first pitch thrown by the legendary Joe DiMaggio.

WILLIE McCOVEY

Like everyone else, San Francisco sportswriters were always highly impressed with the power-hitting ability of big Willie McCovey, whose 521 career home runs earned him election to the Baseball Hall of Fame in 1986, his first year of eligibility. The writers thought much less of McCovey's glovework at first base, but Willie didn't let their low opinions affect his own feelings about his fielding ability.

One day after McCovey had made an outstanding fielding play at first, the writers gathered around his locker. They praised him effusively for a while and then began hinting that they would like to hear his explanation for what they considered to be a performance beyond his capabilities. McCovey completely took the wind out of their sails by saying, "I never said I couldn't field. You guys did."

THE MEXICAN LEAGUE

Ask anybody who's ever been there, and they'll tell you that baseball in the Mexican League is . . . well, different . . . to say the least. Minor league pitcher Tom Puehl spent one year in the Mexican League, and while it didn't advance his career, the stint turned out to be the most unforgettable cultural experience of his life.

"Baseball was a lot different back in the fifties," says Puehl. "I was basically stuck in the minors with no real shot at making the majors because there was so much competition. I belonged to the Brooklyn Dodgers, and back then they had twenty-two teams in their farm system. That's why I wound up going to Mexico in 1955.

"The year before I had pitched for Elmira, New York, in the Eastern League. I'd had a pretty good year—I went 16–7, something like that—and the Eastern League was a pretty tough circuit. A lot of the parent clubs assigned some of their best prospects to their teams in the league, and a lot of guys jumped from the Eastern League right to the majors. But the Dodgers were planning to send me to the Southern Association. When I complained about that, they offered to send me to the Mexican League, which at the time was equivalent to very good Double-A ball or not-so-good Triple-A ball.

"Anyway, I went down there with four other guys from the Dodgers' farm system. Like me, they were tired of not making any progress. We were assigned to the Monterey Sultans. It didn't take long for us to realize that Mexico was a lot different from the U.S. Right before the seventh inning of the very first game we played, some soldiers came out of nowhere—we didn't notice them before—and stood lined up from the bases to the outfield wall on both of the foul lines. We wondered what the heck they were doing there. We found out at the end of the seventh when hundreds of teenagers poured over the fences and ran around the field, screaming and yelling like crazy and raising a cloud of dust over the entire field. The policemen, who were sort of like our National Guard, didn't try to stop them, and after about fifteen minutes the teenagers climbed back over the fences and the game continued. It turned out that this wasn't a fluke but a tradition. It happened every night! The first week we were there I also saw a fan make a perfect swan dive out of the upper deck. He landed on the people below, and apparently nobody, including him, was seriously hurt. Later on I saw an umpire get shot in the middle of a game—he was hit in the arm, so it didn't kill him.

"Even though the Mexican League offered us pretty good competition, it was tough not being able to speak the language. The owner of the Monterey team liked to use his ballplayers to promote the ball club, and one time he asked me to put in an appearance at a dance. I said sure, figuring it would not be a big deal. They fixed me up with a beautiful girl, and the dance turned out to be this very formal affair in a huge ballroom. There must have been five thousand people there. Not knowing one word of Spanish, I had to stand up and make a little speech to that crowd that didn't understand one word of English. To top it off, I also had to lead the dancing, and I'd never even seen a cha-cha before. Talk about feeling like an idiot!

"And then the conditions down there were terrible. We had to make some long road trips, and they were all by bus. They were school buses, too. We were used to better in the United States because the Dodgers always did things first-class. Our first road trip was a long one, to Vera Cruz, and after we got back we complained to the owner of the team, told him we wanted to go by train next time. Our second road trip, to Mérida, Yucatán, was going to be even longer than the first one, and the owner of the team agreed to send us by train. To show you what they thought of their own countrymen, they put the Mexican players in third class while the other four Americans and I got to sit in first class. It didn't really matter, though, because when the train got about ten miles outside of town, it stopped. And there waiting for us was our bus. We got off the train and onto the bus. It took us about a day and a half to get to Mérida. We had a terrible driver who weaved all over the road, and we took turns staying awake to make sure we were still alive.

"The owner of the team thought this little stunt was funny. It was his way of saying, 'You want to travel by train? Okay, I'll give you a train ride.' You have to understand the Mexican sense of humor. If they can swindle you or cheat you or trick you somehow, they don't think it's wrong. They think it's funny. I'll give you another example. One time my paycheck was short. The owner of our ball club also owned a shirt factory, so I went to the factory to talk to him about my paycheck. When I got there, there was a line of about 150 factory workers outside the door to his office. Since I couldn't speak any Spanish, I pantomimed a question to several people in line: 'What are you doing here?' They all pulled out their paychecks and pointed to them. It turned out that everybody in that line had been shorted on their paychecks too! I got into the back of the line to wait my turn, but the owner's daughter walked by and saw me. She said I didn't have to wait in line, and she took me right into her father's office. The owner started laughing as soon as he saw me. He thought it was hilarious, but he paid me what he owed me right away, and he shook my hand and said, 'No hard feelings, eh?'

"Don't get me wrong. I'm glad I went to Mexico and had the experience of playing in the Mexican League, but one year was enough. I was glad to come back to the United States."

MILESTONE BASEBALLS

Saving milestone baseballs is one of the most sacred traditions of major league baseball. Every player's first base hit in the big leagues, for example, is a special, once-in-a-lifetime moment, so to preserve the memory the baseball is taken out of play and tossed to a coach in the dugout. The coach then takes a pen and records the significance of the event on the baseball, which is later presented to the player, who proudly displays it in his trophy case at home. The same thing is done when players reach significant milestones later in their careers, such as a batter knocking out his 100th home run or his 500th base hit, a pitcher recording his 100th win or his 500th strikeout, and so on.

The process does not always go off without a hitch, though. Consider what happened to Barry Larkin of the Reds and Brett Butler of the Giants when they reached certain milestones in their careers.

Larkin was with the Reds in San Diego in May 1997 when he collected his 1,500th base hit; however, no one stopped the game to collect Barry's trophy, and so the ball was kept in play. Reds catcher Eddie Taubensee hit the ball foul down the right-field line, where the Padres' ball girl, Kelly O'Neill, scooped it up and handed it as a goodwill gesture to a fan sitting in the box seats along the railing. The fan asked O'Neill to autograph the souvenir, and she obliged. The Reds finally woke up and retrieved the ball for Larkin, but not in time to keep it from being desecrated. After the game, the embarrassed O'Neill said,

"Please tell him I'm sorry, but maybe my autograph will be worth something someday."

Butler's Giants teammates were more on the ball when he recorded his 1,000th major league hit during a late-July game in 1988 at Candlestick Park against the Los Angeles Dodgers. The milestone hit was quintessential Butler, as the speedy little leadoff hitter and expert bunter beat out an infield hit off the Dodgers' Fernando Valenzuela. The trouble for Butler was that the milestone baseball was not given for documentation and safekeeping to an avuncular coach but to pitcher Mike Krukow, the Giants' resident jokester.

On one side of the ball Krukow dutifully inscribed: "Brett Butler's 1,000th career hit, single."

But then, on the other side of the ball, Krukow wrote: "994th infield single."

THE MINOR LEAGUES

Players in the minor leagues naturally look to the major leagues for ways to improve all facets of their game. Plans to imitate major league strategies and techniques don't always work out, though. Doc Edwards, a congenial West Virginian who has spent more than forty years in baseball as a big league player, manager, coach, and scout, tells the following story about a major league training exercise that backfired in the minor leagues.

"This happened when I was managing the Cleveland Indians' Triple-A club in Charleston, West Virginia. At the time Steve Carlton was getting a lot of publicity out of the conditioning and strength program set up for him by a personal trainer named Gus Hoefling. The most unusual thing about the program was an exercise where Carlton would take his pitching hand, stick it into a five-gallon can of rice, and work his hand all the way down to the bottom of the can, where he would pick up a set of car keys and then work his hand all the way back out of the can. It doesn't sound like much until you try to do it, but then you find out you can hardly do it because it really works all the little muscles in your forearm.

"Well, the pitchers on my club in Charleston heard about this exercise, and they all wanted to do it. I told them, 'Okay, fine. But you can't do it before a game. If you do, your forearm will be too tired, especially after the first time you do it.' The next day was Sunday, and we were going to play an afternoon game. Since we had a night game scheduled for Monday, I figured they could do the exercise after Sunday's game and have plenty of time to rest before Monday night. So we got a can of rice and put it in the clubhouse on Saturday.

"On Saturday night, after everybody had gone home, one of the pranksters on the team slipped into the clubhouse. He scooped about half the rice out of the can, lowered his pants, squatted over the can, and then used it for his toilet. When he was finished, he filled the can back up with rice and left. The next day the pitcher who wanted to go first put his hand into the can and started working. Everybody was gathered around watching him. He was really going at it, digging his fingers into the rice, working his hand deeper and deeper into the rice, until, about halfway down to the bottom, he hit what the prankster had left in the can the night before. You could tell by the look on his face that he knew what it was. When he worked his hand back out, it had rice and you-know-what stuck all over it.

"And that was the end of that program. Nobody trusted that can of rice after that."

In no other sphere of human activity does Murphy's Law ("Everything that can go wrong will go wrong") seem to reign more supremely than in the minor leagues. Tom Venditelli, who played second base (1949–60) in the New York Yankees' and Kansas City Athletics' farm systems, certainly experienced this phenomenon, and he tells a couple of stories about situations where good old Yankee (and Athletic) ingenuity won out over Murphy's Law.

"One time when I was with the Abilene, Texas, ball club we had to go to Corpus Christi to play. Our bus got into town about two or three in the morning, but somebody had screwed up and there were no reservations for us at the hotel we were supposed to be staying at. Worse, there was a regatta in town, and every hotel in the area was completely booked. Our manager, Al Evans, a former catcher for the Washington Senators, got fed up with the desk clerk calling around and having no luck, so he said, 'Screw this. I'm gonna find us a place to stay.' He grabbed the phone, made a couple of calls, and said, 'Back on the bus; we got a place to stay.'

"Our 'place to stay' turned out to be the county jail, and the accommodations were luxurious, let me tell you. The beds were wooden slabs that hung perpendicular to the wall and were held up by two chains that ran from the wall to the edge of the slabs. We slept head to toe, two guys to a slab. We were pretty disgusted, but there was nothing else we could do. Years later I had some fun with my kids by telling them I once spent the night in jail. They didn't believe me until I told them this story."

"Back in 1954 I played with the Norfolk (Virginia) Tars, a Yankees Class-B outfit in the Piedmont League. We drew very good crowds because we had a pennant-winning team and because the general manager promoted like crazy. One of his promotions I'll never forget was swimsuit night. He put an ad in the paper that said the girl with the best figure would win $100.

"Well, on the night of the swimsuit contest, the fans kept coming and coming. They wanted to get a look at all the women in swimsuits, and we must have had a crowd of over ten thousand. The only problem was that only one girl signed up to be in the contest. About an hour before game time the general manager started panicking: 'What the hell am I gonna do?' He fretted a little longer, then said, 'We advertised a swimsuit contest, so we're gonna have a swimsuit contest. I need some volunteers.' He drove over to Sears, bought a bunch of wigs, bras, ladies' shorts and shoes, and hurried back. While he was gone, his wife put all sorts of makeup on us, and when he got back we got dressed for the contest.

"Thank goodness that the one girl who did sign up was Miss Norfolk. She was the first one the general manager introduced. She was a knockout, and when she came prancing out of the dugout in her leopard-skin bathing suit and high heels, the crowd went nuts. I was next in line in the dugout, and since I'm from Providence, Rhode Island, the GM introduced me as 'Miss Rhode Island!' Jim Coates, a big 6'4" pitcher who made it up to the Yankees, came out as 'Miss Virginia.' Bob Rack was 'Miss Missouri'; Moe Thacker was 'Miss Illinois'; and my double-play partner, a Jewish kid from Brooklyn, New York, named Stan Rosenzweig, was 'Miss Brooklyn.' We all looked funny as hell, stumbling around in those high heels and bras, but the funniest of all was Rosey. He was short and stocky, and with hair all over his body he looked like a little bear. We had all stuffed two baseballs into our bras, and as Stan was walking from the dugout toward home plate, he took the balls out, showed them to the crowd, and then put them back in. He called one of his buddies on the other team out of their dugout and then jumped into his arms. When the guy put him down, Stan pulled one of the baseballs out of his bra, tossed it to the guy, and said, 'Why don't you come up and see me some time, big boy!' The fans thought all this was a riot, so what initially looked like it was going to be a big flop turned out to be a helluva night."

Marty Cusack, director of media relations for the Kane County Cougars of the Class-A Midwestern League, also has a story about a promotion that bombed so badly that it turned out to be a fan favorite.

"In the minor leagues, you're always looking for promotions," says Cusack, "but promotions don't always work the way they're supposed to. One of the most unforgettable promotions we ever ran involved a guy who called himself 'Jymmy the Villain,' who told us he was a 'rock 'n' roll magician,' whatever that is. He told us he was going to string a high wire from the press box down to home plate and walk down the high wire, and he was also going to juggle chain saws.

"We booked his act, but then he showed up on the day of the game he was supposed to work and said he couldn't do the high-wire or juggling acts. Instead, he was going to perform a 'leap of death through fire,' as well as karate-chop ten boards in half. At that point we didn't have much choice, so we said okay, do the substitute acts.

"Jymmy had a group of friends to help him, and they were all about eighteen years old. They were dressed in black T-shirts and bandannas. The act started with four of these guys carrying Jymmy in a coffin from the gate in center field in toward the infield around second base. When they reached the infield, they set the coffin upright, and a few seconds later the lid swung open and Jymmy burst out. While another of Jymmy's buddies attempted to build up the act over the PA system, Jymmy started dancing around, doing all sorts of karate moves. Jymmy was wearing a black cape, a Zorro-style hat, and a devil's mask, and there was a mini-trampoline in front of the coffin.

"Meanwhile, two other guys were holding a long two-by-four that had been wrapped in gasoline-soaked rags and set on fire. Jymmy was supposed to jump over this flaming two-by-four by springing off the mini-trampoline, but something got screwed up. The two-by-four had been set on fire too early, or the blaze was bigger than they expected. At any rate, the flames forced the two guys holding the two-by-four to drop it, and when they did the infield grass caught on fire. Even though there was no flaming two-by-four in the air that he had to clear, Jymmy jumped off the trampoline anyway, and when he did he landed right on his butt in the burning infield grass!

"Fortunately, our ground crew sprang into action immediately. They were extremely irritated about the whole thing, but they rushed out onto the field with water hoses and doused the fire. When I saw Jymmy land on his butt, I started laughing so hard I had to leave the press box. I actually didn't see the next part of Jymmy's act, but here's what happened. His friends formed a big circle around him, and he attempted to break the first of about ten boards which were each about a half-inch thick. I think Jymmy dented the board on his first chop; he broke his hand on the second chop, at which point his buddies took him to the hospital. About halfway through the game Jymmy called me from the hospital to say that he wouldn't be able to complete his act after the game.

"The reaction of most people in the crowd that day was either stunned silence or the sort of buzzing fascination usually reserved for *The Jerry Springer Show* or auto race crashes. As bad as Jymmy's act was, it turned out to be a successful promotion, because people were still talking about it three years later, which is what you always want. You can book the greatest act in the world, but if people don't talk about it later, it doesn't do you a whole lot of good.

"As for Jymmy, we've never heard from him again. Did he try to pull a fast one on us? I don't think so. I think he really thought he had an act, that he actually had talent. If he did have it, he sure didn't show it that night."

Ex–minor league second sacker Tommy Venditelli also remembers a Norfolk Tars catcher, not so much for his hustle and considerable ability, but for a stunt he pulled. "The Yankees were hoping this guy would one day take Yogi Berra's place, but he never made it for some reason. When he got sent down to Norfolk from a higher league, he was nice enough but a little aloof. Now, everybody on the team knew where everybody else on the team stayed, but nobody knew where this catcher stayed. We could never get in touch with him away from the ballpark. He finally told us, 'Don't worry about it. I'm staying at the Hotel Mercury.' That was fine, except we couldn't find the Hotel Mercury, because there wasn't one. The Hotel Mercury was his car! For four or five weeks he parked his car at Ocean View Beach on the outskirts of Norfolk and slept in his car every night—the only time he slept in a bed was when we went on the road—until the general manager found out about it and made him rent a room somewhere."

In 1996 *Baseball America* rated Des Moines, Iowa's Sec Taylor Stadium as the sixth-best minor league ballpark in the country, and it's not hard to see why the home of the Triple-A Iowa Cubs deserves such a high ranking. Replacing its old namesake in 1991, the new Sec Taylor Stadium offers a beautiful brick main entrance; an award-winning playing surface; an outstanding gift shop; a large picnic area; a Cubs Club restaurant; forty-four skyboxes; and comfortable, close-to-the-action, unobstructed-view seating for 11,000 fans. As if that weren't enough, there is also Sec Taylor's scenic location, a peninsula at the confluence of the Des Moines and Raccoon Rivers, which gives fans a perfect view (over the center-field wall) of the state capitol building and its twenty-two-karat gold-covered dome.

Because of its location, with woods to the east and west of the site, Sec Taylor also occasionally gives fans a disconcerting view . . . of the skunks that are attracted to the ballpark by the aromas emanating from the concession stands.

As many as fifty skunks per year are caught at Sec Taylor Stadium, but most of them don't get near the fans. Most of the trespassers are caught in metal cages, baited with hot dogs that are strategically placed by members of the ground crew on a grassy knoll behind the right-field wall. When the cagier skunks get past this first line of defense and enter the ballpark proper, they must be cornered and captured with cardboard boxes. The ground crew take pride in their skunk-catching abilities—each man's running total of skunks caught for the year is kept on a tally board in the ground crew equipment building—but when the situation really stinks, it is not the ground crew who are called into action but Phil Horn, a ponytailed, jack-of-all-trades Cubs employee. As Stadium Operations Assistant Jeff Tilley says, "Phil is the skunkmaster, that's for sure."

"The biggest ruckus we ever had was one night when a skunk got down in the box seats and scared about seventy-five people half to death," says Horn. "Some ladies and a few kids were screaming, and nobody else could catch him, so they yelled for me on the radio. When I got there, the ground crew were ready to throw baseballs at him to keep him from getting too close to anybody, but I could see that he was a little guy, probably too young to be able to spray. I think he just wanted to see some of the ball game.

"Anyway, I caught him the way I usually do. I sneaked up behind him with a cardboard box, and then when he noticed me I kept him calm by talking to him in a soft voice, just like you'd talk to a scared kid. Later on, I took him down to Badger Creek and let him go, like I always do.

"I guess the reason I'm so lucky at catching skunks is that I've got eighteen years' experience with them on the farm." Fortunately, Horn has never been sprayed by a skunk. His dog can't say the same thing, though. "It was baaad!" says Horn. "I had to give him a bath in tomato juice and vinegar. That was the only way to get rid of that smell."

Even though Horn does not collect any extra, hazardous-duty pay, the ballpark skunk-catching business has not meant the stench of roadkill for him but the sweet smell of success instead. "I never thought skunk catching would help me at work, but I'm glad it does because I love working here at the ballpark, and I'm hoping they keep me on year-round."

Part of the Mickey Mantle legend, not found in juvenile biographies of the great Yankees slugger, has Mantle hitting a home run while being half drunk or at least extremely hungover. Dick Fitzgerald, who pitched in the Baltimore Orioles' farm system, tells a similar, if not identical, story about a minor league slugger named Joe Taylor.

"Joe Taylor was a great Triple-A ballplayer," says Fitzgerald. "He could do it all. He had a cup of coffee in the big leagues, but he really should have had a career in the majors.

"Anyway, one day in 1959 when Joe and I were on the Vancouver ball club in the PCL, Joe came to the ballpark drunk. We tried to sober him up by getting him to drink a lot of coffee and juice, but that didn't help a whole lot, so when the game started Joe was not in the lineup.

"When the ninth inning rolled around, we were trailing 2 to 1, but we had the tying and winning runs on base with two outs. Joe was feeling better at that point, and he started pestering our manager, Charlie Metro, to let him pinch hit. 'Come on, Charlie. Put me in, and I'll break this thing wide open.'

"Metro pinch hit him, and Joe struck out on three pitches. Three fastballs right down the middle, and Joe didn't even take the bat off his shoulder.

"Of course, Metro was pissed. And as he started walking down the concrete corridor to our locker room, Joe came up behind him and said, 'Charlie, you dumb ass. . . . You knew I was drunk. Why'd you put me in?'"

VINEGAR BEND MIZELL

Wilmer David Mizell came by his nickname geographically. According to the big left-handed pitcher, the population of his hometown of Vinegar Bend, Alabama, was only 37 when he was born there. Certainly, Mizell has been the only Vinegar Bend native son to graduate to the big leagues.

Although control problems prevented Mizell from ever becoming much more than a .500 pitcher, he did spend nine years in the major leagues (most of them with the St. Louis Cardinals), and he made a brief appearance with the Pittsburgh Pirates in the 1960 World Series. After baseball Mizell kept the name of his hometown current by serving several terms as a Republican congressman from Mississippi. No doubt Mizell's "country-style" sense of humor enlivened many an otherwise tedious congressional meeting. For instance, when talking about the Mizell family living conditions when he was growing up, Mizell once said, "One day a fire started in the bathroom, but we were able to put it out before it reached the house."

Mizell also has a repertory of humorous baseball stories, including the following umpire yarn.

"You know, there's one man on the baseball field who can be right only fifty percent of the time: the umpire.

"In my time I've heard a lot of good remarks made to umpires. But I believe the best one I ever heard was when I was with the St. Louis Cardinals. It occurred one day when I was pitching and Hal Smith was catching. That day we had this big tall umpire behind the plate, and he towered over Smitty, who was only five foot nine.

"Now, most of the time when Smitty was catching we got our share of close pitches. That pitch that's knee high on the outside corner or letter high on the inside corner . . . believe me, you need those pitches in the big leagues.

"The umpires liked Smitty. He always referred to them respectfully, using their right names, and they appreciated that. But this one afternoon we didn't feel that we were getting our share of close pitches, so Smitty kept jawing back and forth with the home-plate umpire as the game wore on. Finally, in the eighth inning with the tying run at third base, two men out, and two balls and two strikes on a good right-handed hitter, I threw what I thought was a perfect strike . . . right down the middle. And the umpire said, 'Ball.'

"Well, Smitty jumped up and turned around to the umpire—which you're not supposed to do under any circumstances—and said, 'Ball!?! How in the world could you call that pitch a ball?'

"The umpire said, 'You turn around and squat back down, Shorty, before I bite your head off.'

"And Smitty said, 'If you do, you'll have more brains in your stomach than you've got in your head!'

"Like I said, I think that was the best comeback I've ever heard a ballplayer make to an umpire, but unfortunately it came with a price. We had to finish the game that day without Smitty."

JOHN MONTEFUSCO

San Francisco Giants pitcher John Montefusco was one of the most colorful players of the 1970s because of his penchant for making outrageous predictions and then backing them up. Montefusco's braggadocio surfaced early and served him well. At Middletown (New Jersey) Township High School, Montefusco was a weak-hitting shortstop who didn't impress a single baseball scout, at least not with his playing ability. The scouts didn't exactly knock down his door when he took up pitching in community college either, but Montefusco persuaded scout Frank Burke to sign him in 1973 and then immediately told Burke he would be in the big leagues within two years. Burke and the entire Giants organization were astounded when the brash Montefusco made good on his boast, as the right-handed fastballer earned his ticket to San Francisco at the end of the 1974 season after pitching superbly in the minor leagues at Decatur, Amarillo, and Phoenix. The following year Montefusco won the National League Rookie of the Year Award by going 15–9, with a 2.88 ERA and 215 strikeouts (good for second in the league). He also began attracting widespread notoriety for his self-fulfilling prophecies, promising to shut out the Los Angeles Dodgers and then doing so, 1–0.

Injuries later curtailed Montefusco's effectiveness with the Giants, and he was traded to the Atlanta Braves in 1981, then from the Braves to the San Diego Padres in 1982. But he never lost his supreme self-confidence, as the following story told by Padres pitcher Chris Welsh illustrates.

"I was in my second year in the big leagues in 1982," says Welsh, "and I was one of several very young pitchers on the Padres. We were all impressed with John because he had achieved some fame as a feared fastballer with the Giants.

"Now, as you may know, every time a professional baseball team begins a new series with a different team, the pitchers and catchers get together for a meeting to go over the hitters on the other team. Every hitter in the other team's lineup is covered, and you hear things like 'This guy likes to hit the first pitch,' 'So-and-so can hit-and-run,' 'Don't throw a high fastball to Joe Blow.' After a while, all these meetings start to sound alike, and the consensus among players is that if you've been to one of these meetings you've been to them all; however, at the time, because we were all so young, we weren't so cynical and blasé about the meetings as we would later become.

"So, there we were, going into Philadelphia to face the Phillies, who back then had a pretty significant lineup, with guys like Pete Rose, Manny Trillo, Mike Schmidt, Gary Matthews, Garry Maddox, Bo Diaz. We were having our meeting to go over these hitters, and our pitching coach, Norm Sherry, was directing the meeting. He had notes about each hitter written on three-by-five cards, and he would frequently refer to the note cards.

"Norm said, 'Okay, the Phillies lead off with Pete Rose. He's a switch-hitter, so he'll be hitting lefty today since Montefusco's pitching. He's a fastball hitter who likes the ball down and in but is tough to fool with breaking stuff. He's disciplined at the plate and won't chase many bad pitches. He hits the ball to all fields,' . . . blah, blah, blah. 'John, how you going to pitch Rose?'

"Montefusco said, 'I'm going to blow 'im away!'

"Sherry looked up from his cards and said, 'What do you mean?'

"Montefusco said, 'Just what I said, I'm going to blow 'im away.'

"Norm hesitated for a second, but then went on. 'Okay, Manny Trillo hits second. He's another contact hitter who hits the ball where it's pitched,' . . . blah, blah, blah. 'How you gonna pitch Trillo, John?'

"'I'm going to blow 'im away!'

"'How you going to pitch Matthews?'

"'Gonna blow 'im away!'

"'And Mike Schmidt?'

"'Gonna blow 'im away! . . . Screw it! I'm gonna blow 'em all away!' After saying that, Montefusco stood up and walked out of the meeting. As he did, Sherry threw his index cards up in the air in exasperation, and that was the end of the meeting. The rest of us pitchers looked around at each other and were thinking, 'Great. Now what are we mere mortals going to do?'"

JERRY MORALES

Surrendering home runs may be an occupational hazard of pitching, but when a pitcher gets too generous with the long ball his teammates are certain to make fun of it. Ex–New York Mets pitcher John Pacella remembers what happened when Mets outfielder Jerry Morales continually derided their teammate Mark Bomback for the excessive number of homers he allowed during the 1980 season.

"Mark had a decent year on the mound for us in 1980, but he gave up a lot of home runs, something like thirty-five of them, and Morales was constantly agitating him about it. Morales called Bomback 'Boom-Boom,' and he would say things like, 'You pitching tonight, Boom-Boom? Yeah? Well, then, I gotta back up against the wall. . . . I gotta play with one arm up on the wall tonight!' Morales said stuff like this all the time, and it almost got to the point of being malicious, but Bomby was a very laid-back guy, fortunately, and he was always able to laugh it off.

"In one of the last games of the season, we were playing the Cubs at Shea Stadium. At some point Leon Durham mashed a home run off of Bomby that went over the right-field wall and also over the wall at the back of our bullpen, where it crashed through the windshield of a brand-new white Camaro Z28. The ball completely destroyed the windshield and landed right in the driver's seat. The funny thing is, as you've probably guessed, the car belonged to Morales.

"I was one of the guys sitting in the bullpen, and we heard the windshield shatter. After the game a security guard came into the clubhouse to tell Morales that his car had been hit, but we told him to keep quiet about it and not to move the baseball out of the front seat. We all walked out with Morales toward his car, and at first he didn't even notice what had happened. When he got up closer and saw the car, he was almost speechless. He said, 'What the . . . ? What the . . . ? He called over the security guard, who was already laughing. Somebody pointed at the front seat and said, 'Hey, Jerry, look what Durham left you.'

"Morales then said, 'You gotta be kidding me! Boom-Boom! Look at this. You gotta keep the ball in the ballpark!'

"The baseball gods really dispensed some beautiful poetic justice that day. Morales gave Bomby grief all year long, but Bomby got in the last laugh."

THURMAN MUNSON

Few players ever made a more lasting impression on team-mates and opponents alike than Thurman Munson, the fiery catcher who was the spiritual leader of the New York Yankees from 1970 until his death in a plane crash halfway though the 1979 season.

Dan Briggs and John Pacella, who run the Big League Base-ball School in Columbus, Ohio, tell stories that attest to both the intensity of Munson's personality and the power of his legacy.

"Munson was one of the greatest competitors I ever saw," says Briggs. "He wasn't ever very friendly with anybody on the other team, but he especially didn't like you if you were beating him and the Yankees.

"One day I was leading off third base, and Munson, who had a good arm and liked to use it, tried to pick me off. I let the ball hit me in the hip, it rolled away, and I was able to run home and score on the play. The next time I came to bat, Munson called for nothing but curveballs from the Yankees' pitcher, Dick Tidrow. Each one of those three curves must have broken thirty feet, and every time I swung and missed, Munson shook his fist in the air and screamed, 'YEAH!' like the Yankees had just won the World Series.

"Another time, we were playing the Yankees in the last game of the regular season, right before their playoff game with Boston. Munson came into the game hitting .298. Naturally, he really wanted to get a couple of hits so that he'd finish the sea-son with a .300 average. He hit a dying quail down the right-

field line, but I ran in and made a sliding catch to rob him of the base hit. Boy, was he pissed!

"The next spring Cleveland traded me out of the American League to San Diego, and the great thing about that was that it got me the hell away from Thurman Munson."

Although he had been dead a couple of years by the time ex–New York Mets pitcher John Pacella realized his childhood dream of playing for the Yankees, Munson still had an impact on Pacella's rocky initiation into pinstripes.

"In 1982 I got traded late in spring training to the Yankees," says Pacella. "The Yankees took me and Mike Morgan north as the tenth and eleventh pitchers on the staff. On Opening Day I was in awe of being in Yankee Stadium and seeing the monuments out in center field. Before the game I was in the outfield shagging flies right next to my childhood hero, Bobby Murcer, and I started having twelve-year-old flashbacks. I had to tell myself, 'Hey, you're a veteran. Calm down.' On top of that, the Yankee fans started riding me unmercifully, yelling stuff like, 'Pacella, you bum, you're a rag-arm traitor!'

" 'People, I'm a New York boy. I was born in Brooklyn. I am thrilled to be here. I've been a Yankee fan all my life,' I said, but it didn't matter. There is such hatred and animosity between Mets and Yankees fans that even though I had become a Yankee, because I had once been a Met, they hated me.

"After the game, I took my shower and then looked for an outlet in my locker for my hair dryer. They were redoing all the lockers, and I couldn't find an outlet in mine, so I got up and walked around until I found an empty locker. There was a bat and a jersey in the locker, but I pushed them out of the way, sat down in a chair facing the mirror in the back of the locker, plugged in my hair dryer, and started blow-drying my hair.

"A couple of minutes later I noticed that a bunch of guys were standing in front of the locker, watching me. It was guys like Graig Nettles, Dave Righetti, Goose Gossage . . . six or seven of 'em, and they weren't smiling. One of them said, 'Do you know whose locker you're sitting in?' And all of a sudden it came to me. I looked up to double-check, and sure enough, his name-plate was still across the top of the locker: Thurman Munson. 'I'm sorry! I didn't know!' I blurted. And to myself I said, 'Geez, what else can go wrong for me today!'"

MASANORI MURAKAMI

Years before Hideo Nomo fever rocked Japan and the Japanese-American communities in the United States, Masanori Murakami caused a similar sensation by becoming the first Japanese to play in the American major leagues. A young left-handed pitcher, Murakami performed well for the San Francisco Giants during the 1964 and 1965 seasons, but a complicated contract dispute between the Giants and the Nankai Hawks of the Japanese Pacific League forced Murakami to return to Japan to finish his professional baseball career.

Like the typical Japanese, Murakami was extremely polite and respectful, and American fans found very endearing his habit of doffing his cap and bowing deeply at the waist in appreciation of a teammate's good fielding play.

Unlike Nomo and other Japanese players in the big leagues today, Murakami did not have an interpreter constantly at his side, and the wise guys on the Giants decided to have a little fun with Murakami's inability to speak or understand English. Cognizant of the Japanese respect for authority, they thought it imperative to teach Murakami what to say in the event that Giants manager Herman Franks needed to relieve him. The situation did indeed occur, and when Franks strode out to the mound and reached out for the baseball from his pitcher, Murakami politely said, "Take a hike, Herman."

NAMES AND NUMBERS

In case you haven't noticed, baseball has something for everyone. No matter what one's nonbaseball interest is, you can bet that baseball somehow has a connection to it. Take names, for instance. An entire book could be written about nothing but baseball nicknames, and in fact a couple of such books have already been published. And if you just like to play around with names, baseball is fertile ground. The longest baseball surname? That would be "Raffensberger," as in pitcher Ken (1939–54), who checks in at thirteen letters. Looking for a surname that's a palindrome? Take your pick between pitcher Dave Otto (1987–94) and shortstop Toby Harrah (1969–86). The first name in the baseball alphabet and in *The Baseball Encyclopedia*? That honor goes, appropriately, to the great Hank Aaron. Fans also love to make up entire lineups of players whose names (first, last, or nickname) connect them by a common subject or theme.

With every new season and fresh crop of rookies there are additional opportunities to have some more fun with baseball names. When the Cincinnati Reds brought a young pitcher named Eddie Priest up to the big show from their Triple-A Indianapolis farm team in late May of 1998, Cincinnatians joked that the last-place Reds were at death's door since a priest had been called in to administer the sacrament of "last rites," or extreme unction. Sportswriter Scott MacGregor was also quick to seize on the religious connotation in the rookie's name. Pointing out that pitchers Howie Nunn (1961–62), Bubba Church (1951–53), and Randy St. Claire (1988) have also worn a

Cincinnati uniform, MacGregor dubbed the rookie part of the Reds' "Holy Quartet" of a priest, nun, church, and saint.

Coincidentally, the name "Bubba Church" figured in some even more clever baseball name wordplay employed by baseball artist Tim Swartz. At Gallery 53's sixteenth annual Fine Arts Look at Baseball show, which kicked off just prior to the 1997 Hall of Fame Induction Weekend in Cooperstown, New York, Swartz exhibited a painting with a puzzling title. The oblong painting consists of two rows of four square boxes, each box being the portrait of a former major leaguer. The eight players seem to have no connection until one carefully considers the piece's title and contemplates the names of the players, reading first (left to right) the names of the players in the top row of boxes and then reading (left to right) the names of the players in the bottom row of boxes, at which point the meaning of the title and the painting's humor is revealed: "Church Shocker, Parsons Moon Parish Duren Easter Service."

Major league players did not always wear numbers on the backs of their uniforms. The Cleveland Indians were the first team to experiment with uniform numbers, in 1916, while the New York Yankees were the first team to permanently adopt numbers on both home and away uniforms, in 1929. Furthermore, although both the American and National Leagues formally required their members to number their uniforms in the early 1930s, it wasn't until 1937 that the Philadelphia A's became the last team to completely comply. According to Harold C. Burr (*Baseball Magazine*, August 1939), it took so long to standardize this simple element of baseball dress that we take for granted today because both owners and players were opposed to it.

Baseball owners thought that putting numbers on players' uniforms would ruin their scorecard business, while players felt that uniform numbers would make them look like convicts.

Most uniform numbers are assigned rather randomly, but some assignments have interesting stories behind them.

Bill Voiselle, a pitcher for the old Boston Braves, is the only player to wear the name of his hometown on the back of his uniform. Voiselle wore number 96 because he was from the little town of Ninety-six, South Carolina.

Chicago White Sox outfielder Carlos May was born May 17, 1948. From 1969 to 1976 Carlos wore number 17; when the White Sox put players' names on the backs of their uniforms from 1969 to 1970, and again briefly in 1976, May was able to wear his birthday on his back.

Born in Honolulu, Hawaii, pitcher Sid Fernandez wore number 50 to honor his home state.

When Barry Bonds broke in with the Pittsburgh Pirates in 1989, he did not take number 25, the number worn by his father, Bobby Bonds, but number 24, which was the number made famous by Barry's godfather and his dad's teammate on the San Francisco Giants, Willie Mays. Although number 24 had been retired by the Giants by the time Barry left Pittsburgh for San Francisco in 1993, Mays generously offered to "unretire" his number so that Barry could wear it. Barry respectfully declined the offer and finally went with number 25 to honor his father.

It's certainly no accident that Colorado Rockies slugger Larry Walker wears number 33. Walker, you see, has a serious superstitious fixation on the number 3. For instance, he goes through a variety of rituals, such as practice swings in the on-deck circle, that involve the number 3 or numbers divisible by 3, and he married Christa Vandenbrink on November 3, 1991, at 3:33 P.M.

Rickey Henderson has worn several different numbers during his long career, but he has become so attached to number

24 that he has bribed new teammates on at least two occasions to give that number to him. Ron Hassey of the Oakland A's swapped his number 24 to Henderson for a couple of expensive suits, while the Toronto Blue Jays' Turner Ward held out for a pair of cowboy boots and a few bats. (He may have been only kidding, but Henderson said that he couldn't play well if he wasn't wearing number 24 on his back.)

Apparently, number 28 held little sentimental value for Phillies outfielder John Kruk, who swapped it to reliever Mitch Williams for two cases of beer. Then again, given his reputation, two cases of free beer may have seemed like the deal of the century to Kruk. A woman once told Kruk that he looked overweight and out of shape for an athlete. Kruk's reply was "I ain't an athlete, lady; I'm a baseball player."

And finally, to pay tribute to Jackie Robinson on the fiftieth anniversary of Robinson's major league debut, Seattle Mariners star Ken Griffey, Jr., wore Robinson's number 42 in a 1997 game against the Cleveland Indians instead of his usual number 24. The next day, acting baseball commissioner Bud Selig announced that to honor Robinson, no player in the major leagues would ever be issued number 42 again. Twelve players who were wearing the number at the time thus became the last of the 42s: Dennis Cook (Marlins), Tom Goodwin (Royals), Butch Huskey (Mets), Mike Jackson (Indians), Scott Karl (Brewers), Jose Lima (Astros), Mariano Rivera (Yankees), Kirk Rueter (Giants), Marc Sagmoen (Rangers), Jason Schmidt (Pirates), Mo Vaughn (Red Sox), and Lenny Webster (Orioles).

BOBO NEWSOM

Often called "the Dizzy Dean of the American League," Bobo Newsom of Hartsville, South Carolina, was one of baseball's zaniest characters. Like ol' Diz, ol' Bobo was a supremely confident braggart who was often able to back up his boasting. Unfortunately, while he was a good pitcher and a fierce competitor, Newsom usually played on bad ball clubs, and he always seemed to have more than his share of bad luck. In 1934, for instance, Bobo pitched a nine-inning no-hitter but lost the game 2–1 in the tenth inning with two outs. (On the other hand, Bobo was once losing a game 15–0 and he said, "How can anyone win with no runs?") He was a 20-game winner three times, but he also led the American League in losses four times. Overall, he won 211 big league games, but that impressive total was offset by 222 losses, making him and Jack Powell the only 200-game winners with losing records in major league history.

While Dean's mastery on the mound made him too valuable a pitcher to trade despite his antics (at least as long as he was healthy), Newsom was often able to wear out his welcome. In fact, Bobo Newsom was the quintessential journeyman ballplayer. Newsom pitched for nine different major league and eight different minor league teams between 1929 and 1953. In the majors he pitched for the Cubs, Red Sox, Tigers, Yankees, and Giants, and enjoyed two different tours of duty with the Philadelphia A's and the Brooklyn Dodgers, three with the St. Louis Browns, and five with the Washington Senators! Seven different times Newsom played for two major league teams during the same season, and in 1943 he played for three major league teams. This constant moving around made it difficult for Newsom to remember names, so he gave up and called everybody, from batboys to club owners, "Bobo."

Newsom was so colorful that he even appealed to the literate John Lardner, who told a couple of memorable Bobo stories in the *True Baseball Yearbook* of 1957.

In 1938 Newsom had a great year for the hapless St. Louis Browns. While the seventh-place Browns won only 55 games all year, Bobo won 20 of the 55. According to Lardner, Bobo started his fine season in a typically zany way. Browns owner Don Barnes promised to buy Newsom a new suit of clothes if he won for the Browns on Opening Day. Newsom did indeed pitch the Brownies to an Opening Day win, so after the game Barnes went up to Newsom, stuffed a wad of money into his hand, and told him to go out and buy himself the suit. "Keep the sugar, Bobo," Newsom said. "Bobo bought the suit before the game. The bill for it is on your desk."

Two years later Newsom had the best year of his career, for the Detroit Tigers. By the All-Star break Newsom had won 13 games on his way to a 21–5 season, with a 2.83 ERA plus two wins and a heartbreaking 2–1, seventh-game loss in the World Series. Bobo was picked to represent the American League in the All-Star Game, but he quit the team when New York Yankees manager Joe McCarthy announced that the AL starting pitcher would be the Yankees' Red Ruffing. Said Newsom: "If I don't start, I don't pitch. Bobo follows nobody."

Newsom rejoined the team when he learned that McCarthy planned to pitch him after Ruffing and before the great Bob Feller, but he still had some audacious advice for McCarthy, telling him: "If you had the brains of a motherless shoat, Bo, you would pitch Bobo all the way." Although Joe Cronin actually wound up managing the American League squad, McCarthy must have been chagrined nevertheless with the results turned in by the AL hurlers. In their 4–0 victory, the National Leaguers scored three runs off Ruffing, one off Feller, and none off Newsom in his three innings of work.

After Newsom retired, a youngster asked him one day how many no-hitters he pitched in the major leagues. "Just the one," Bobo replied. "They don't grow in bunches like bananas, son."

PHIL NIEKRO

Baseball has an old saying that goes, "You don't want a knuckleballer pitching for you, and you don't want a knuckleballer pitching against you." This saying adroitly expresses the ambivalence that many baseball people feel toward the pitch that is the toughest for pitchers to throw, for catchers to catch, and for many batters to hit. Phil Niekro mastered the knuckleball, but he had no easy time doing it.

Niekro grew up in the small coal-mining town of Lansing, Ohio, on the Ohio–West Virginia border, and his father, who pitched in the area's amateur coal miners' league, taught him to throw the knuckler. As a youngster Niekro worked constantly on perfecting the pitch, and he played countless hours of catch in the Niekro backyard with his father, mother, sister, and brother Joe, who also became a knuckleballing major league pitcher. Phil thought he would be signed out of high school, but he wasn't. Undiscouraged, he pitched in the same coal miners' league as his father and eventually attracted the attention of the Milwaukee Braves, who signed him to a professional contract and sent him to the organization's lowest minor league rung. At Wellsville, New York, in 1959 Niekro pitched so poorly that the manager of the ball club was forced to release him. When Niekro bawled his eyes out, the Wellsville manager took pity on him and finagled a spot for him on the roster of the Braves' other Class-D ball club, in McCook, Nebraska. Niekro went 7–1 for McCook and saved his career. For the next five years Niekro steadily progressed through the Braves' minor league system, yet several times Braves scouts and coaches rec-

ommended that the kid with the goofy pitch be released. They simply could not see past the numerous wild pitches, passed balls, walks, and broken catcher's fingers that resulted from Niekro's pitching.

After a couple of trials, Niekro finally made the major leagues for good in 1967. He continued to work at controlling his knuckleball, but at times he seemed to lose his grip, such as the four-year period when he lost 20, 18, 20, and 18 games. Nevertheless, when Niekro's twenty-year major league career was over, it was clear that he had on balance turned in a Hall of Fame performance. A five-time All-Star and five-time Gold Glove winner, Niekro pitched a no-hitter, racked up 3,342 strikeouts (compared to 1,809 bases on balls), and finished with a 318–274 record and an ERA of 3.35.

Niekro was inducted into the Baseball Hall of Fame in the summer of 1997. At the press conference following the induction ceremonies, a youngster who had been credentialed so that he could cover the event for a kids' television program was recognized and allowed to ask Niekro a question. It was a question for which Niekro's entire life was the perfect answer.

"I play Little League baseball and hope to make the major leagues someday. Do you have any advice for Little Leaguers like me?" asked the youngster.

"I never played Little League baseball," said Niekro, "but the best advice I can give you is . . . Practice, practice, practice. . . . And when you think you're good enough, practice some more. . . . And then, when you think you're as good as you can be, practice some more."

JOHN PACELLA

John Pacella was a right-handed pitcher who appeared in seventy-four games for the Mets, Yankees, Twins, Orioles, and Tigers during parts of six seasons between 1977 and 1986. Pacella also spent a season on the roster of the Tokyo Giants—an arm injury prevented him from actually pitching in a game in Japan—and he later managed the Newark Bisons, Rio Grande Whitewings, and Kalamazoo Kodiaks, three independent minor league teams. Along with his partner Dan Briggs, he now owns and operates the Big League Baseball School, a year-round baseball instructional school in Columbus, Ohio.

Despite Pacella's considerable baseball experience, he is remembered mostly for one thing: the way his cap fell off his head after every pitch he delivered. Pacella was a fastball pitcher, and in putting everything he had into every pitch he threw, he violently jerked his head down and to the left as he released the ball.

"I don't remember exactly when it started," says Pacella, "but I do know that in high school I developed a rhythm to deal with it: I'd throw, my hat would fall off, and I'd pick it up and put it back on my head . . . all in one motion. It didn't slow the game down one bit, and I wouldn't have thought twice about it if people hadn't constantly asked me about it.

"Yes, believe it or not, one time a batted ball did go into my hat. It happened in the minors, and a hard-hit grounder took my hat all the way out to the second baseman. The second baseman grabbed my hat and tossed it aside, then picked up the ball and threw the batter out at first. That was nothing, though, compared to the problem I had, or almost had, in the majors. One day when I was slated to be the starting pitcher for the Mets against the Dodgers, I was sitting in front of my locker about twenty minutes before game time, mentally preparing myself to pitch the game. Our manager, Joe Torre, came over to me and said, 'I don't know if I can start you tonight.'

" 'Why not?' I asked him.

" 'A couple of protests have been made about your hat always flying off when you pitch. Some guys are claiming that your hat falling off is a major distraction.'

"I found out later that some guys on the Cubs and Ron Cey, the Dodgers' third baseman, were the protesters. 'Well, can I just pitch with no hat at all?' I asked Torre.

" 'I don't know,' said Torre. 'We'll check with the commissioner.' And they did. They got on the phone with Bowie Kuhn's office, and the answer was no, I had to be in full uniform. They got back on the phone and talked some more about what to do about the situation. While they were talking, the Mets' clubhouse manager tried to help me out by making me a couple of caps with chin straps. He took the Mets caps and sewed a strip of hard elastic onto each of them. The chin straps kept these caps on my head, but they puffed out my cheeks and made them look swollen, as if the dentist had just pulled out a couple of my teeth. When Torre saw me in one of the caps, he just frowned and shook his head slightly, as if to say, 'There's no way you're going out there like that.' On the other hand, Marv Albert, the sportscaster, thought they were a hoot and took one to keep as a souvenir.

"I guess the commissioner disallowed the protest in the end because I went ahead and pitched the game the way I always did, but the hat falling off remained an issue. In my locker at Shea Stadium I had a shoe box full of letters from fans suggesting things I could do to keep my cap on my head. One guy suggested I use pine tar; another guy said Velcro strips; and another guy said I should bobby-pin it on. Every day I got a new suggestion, and a lot of them were from nuts, like the guy who said I should put a nail in my head. One guy actually threatened me because he felt I was 'a mockery to baseball and shouldn't be allowed to pitch in the major leagues.'

"It wasn't just the fans who always seemed to bring it up, either. One time Ralph Kiner was interviewing me on the "Star of the Game" show and he said, 'John, you pitched a terrific game tonight, and we'll talk about that in a minute, but we've got to ask you first: Why does your hat fall off?' I told him about my delivery and added that 'my head is an odd, in-between size, and they just don't seem to make caps in my size.' Another time I was batting against the Reds, and Johnny Bench said, 'Your helmet's not going to fly off when you swing, is it?'

"There was a guy who worked for the advertising agency that handled the Mets, and he told me one time, 'Don't even try to stop your hat from falling off, because after you leave the game, that's what people are going to remember you for.' At the time I thought he was wrong, thought it was a silly thing to say, but time has proven him to be exactly right. Baseball fans, especially Mets fans, remember me as the pitcher whose cap always fell off."

It's no secret that most baseball players love the game of golf and play a round or two every chance they get. Pacella tells a story about a time when he definitely should not have ventured out on the links.

"In 1977, when I was twenty-one years old, I was on the Mets' major league roster for the first time during spring training. It was the second week of spring training, and I was still pretty nervous and unsure of myself. I was just trying to go with the flow.

"One day I was sitting at my locker when I noticed two very official-looking guys going around to each locker, asking each guy on the team if he wanted to play in this big charity golf tournament that they held each year in St. Petersburg. I knew this tournament was a big deal—it was televised and everything—because the guys had already been talking about it for days. As these two guys got closer to my locker I wondered if they were going to talk to me.

"Sure enough, they stopped at my locker. 'Oh, John Pacella, you're the young pitcher. How ya doing! John, do you play golf?'

"I play golf now, but at that point in time I had never even held a golf club in my hands. My inner voice said, 'Bail out right now!' but I didn't listen. I was afraid to say no, afraid that if I did I'd look like an oddball, so I said, 'Yeah, I play golf.'

" 'Great, we're happy to have you,' the guy said, and just like that I was signed up to play in this big tournament that ballplayers from all over Florida were coming to play in.

" 'You got your clubs with you?' the guy asked.

" 'No, I didn't bring 'em down,' I said. Again, my inner voice tried to tell me: 'You're a stupid ass. You should bail out now.'

" 'Don't worry,' the guy said, 'we can lend you a set of clubs. . . . What's your handicap?'

" 'My handicap? Does the guy think I've got a busted ankle or a sore arm?' I wondered.

" 'Your handicap, what's your handicap?' he asked me again. 'Are you a scratch golfer?'

"I had no idea what the guy was talking about, so I didn't answer him. Then he said, 'What are you, eight, nine, ten?'

" 'Yeah, ten,' I said, figuring a higher number would be better than a lower number.

" 'All right, I'll put you down as a ten. We need to know for the pairings. It's a scramble, you know.'

" 'Oh, sure,' I said, although I didn't have a clue what the guy was talking about. 'Hey, when is this thing?' I asked.

" 'In two weeks,' the guy said. 'I hope you're still with the team then so you can play in the tourney.'

" 'Yeah, me too,' I said, although I was now secretly hoping that I'd get sent down to the minors so I wouldn't have to play in it.

"Almost two weeks later, a couple of days before the tournament, the two guys were back in our clubhouse. The guy I talked to before came over and asked, 'You still playing?'

" 'Yeah.'

" 'Have you hit any yet?'

" 'Nope.'

" 'Well, here's your information packet.' The envelope had stuff in it like a program, my tee time, directions to the golf course, the names of the guys in my group. 'You got shoes with you?'

" 'Yeah, I got shoes,' I said, but that was a big lie, so the day before the tournament I went to a sporting goods store and spent a hundred dollars on a brand-new pair of brown patent leather golf shoes.

"I had to be at the golf course at seven-thirty in the morning. As I got near the entrance and saw a long line of cars, TV trucks, and people all over the place, it started to dawn on me how big a deal this thing was. A girl waved me into the celebrity parking lot, and after I parked my car I headed over to the clubhouse. I had no clubs and no golf balls, but I did have my brand-new shoes, which I was still carrying around in the box. They had a loaner set of clubs ready for me, and I bought two sleeves of balls, six balls total. 'I won't need more than that,' I thought. The guy in the pro shop asked me if I needed a golf glove, and I said yes I did, a right-handed glove. That was the wrong glove to get, because it put the glove on my top hand.

"I found the guys I was playing with: Garth Iorg, Ken and Clete Boyer, and I noticed right away that I wasn't dressed the way they were. They all had on nice Ban-Lons, while I was wearing a T-shirt. They all had golf gloves on their bottom hand, while I was wearing a glove on my top hand. Worst of all, they all were wearing short socks that hardly came above their golf shoes, while I was wearing baseball sanitary socks that came up to my knees. 'I look like hell,' I thought. I pushed my socks down, but they didn't look any better bunched up around my ankles. I thought about trying to cut them off at the ankles, but I couldn't think of what I could have used to cut them with.

"The organizers had everybody in their groups by this time, and they were starting to disperse the groups. I was thinking, 'I've got to ask somebody what a scramble is,' when we were told that we would be the first group to tee off.

"I had the highest handicap in my group, so the guys told me to hit first. I had been nervous all along, but now I got scared because I could see that there were a thousand spectators lined up on both sides of the first tee. Big names like Willie Mays and Tom Seaver were being interviewed nearby, and people were taking pictures. I was the first guy up in the whole tournament, and I had never swung at a golf ball in my life. I didn't even know how to hold a club, but it was too late to turn back. I gave the guys in my group another hint that I didn't know what the heck I was doing when I bent over to put my tee into the grass, stood up, and then bent down again to put my ball on the tee. I took one practice swing, then hit the ball. I hit a slice that was an absolute bullet. It went about sixty yards and veered into the crowd. I can remember watching, as if it happened in slow motion, the crowd part like the Red Sea. People were diving to the right and diving to the left to get out of the way, but I could see that an old lady was not going to make it. Just as she turned, the ball hit her right in the back and knocked her down. 'Oh, God, I've killed some 180-year-old lady at a golf tournament!' I thought. One of the tournament officials waved at us, as if to say that the lady was going to be okay, and the guys in my group said, 'That's all right. Don't worry about it.' I was thinking, 'Do I hit another shot, or is that one okay?'

"The other guys in my group all hit their first shots about three hundred yards straight down the fairway, so we were about a hundred and fifty yards short of the green. The guys were asking, 'What are you going to hit, a six-iron or a nine?' I looked at the numbers on my clubs and thought, 'How the hell do you tell which one is the six and which one is the nine?'

"I was the first to putt, and because the green had a big break to the right, my ball didn't come anywhere near the hole. Somebody sneered, 'That was a good read,' and I thought, 'Uh-oh, they're definitely onto me now.'

"By the third hole nobody in the group was even talking to me. They all hated me, and they were thinking, 'This guy's brutal! Why is he even playing in the tournament?' I was down to two balls, and I thought, 'Geez, I'm going to need some more balls.' My brand-new shoes, which were as stiff as a board, were killing my feet and the backs of my ankles. I was already walking on my toes, and when I looked down at my feet I saw blood running up my sanitary socks.

"The third hole was a short par four. When we were about eighty yards away, I thought about using my wedge but hit my four-iron instead. I hit it well, too. It went about a hundred seventy yards and flew over the heads of the people on the next hole. I think that that would have been the last straw anyway, but one of the guys noticed my socks and said, 'Hey, your feet are bleeding. Maybe you ought to call it a day.'

" 'Yeah, I guess so,' I said, 'I'm out of balls anyway. But I can't walk in. Somebody will have to drive me in. When I got to the clubhouse and took off my shoes, I saw that my socks inside the shoes were completely soaked in blood.

"The next day I dreaded going into the Mets' clubhouse. My feet were so sore that I could hardly even walk, and I knew the guys were going to give me some grief. Our second baseman, Doug Flynn, said, 'John, how'd you hit yesterday?' And our manager, Joe Torre, said, 'I heard you have one helluva slice!' I deserved the kidding, though, because I had to go and try to be a big shot. It was the stupidest thing I've ever done in my life, and it taught me a lesson: that there are certain things in life you just can't bluff; that if you try, people will know immediately that you're bluffing; and that playing golf is one of those things you just can't bluff."

TED POWER

A big, strong, hard-throwing right-hander, Ted Power was signed out of Kansas State University by the Los Angeles Dodgers. Even though Power was outstanding for the Dodgers' Triple-A farm team—Ted went 18–3 for the 1981 Albuquerque Dukes—there just wasn't room for him on the Dodgers' talented and experienced pitching staff, and he was traded to Cincinnati in October 1982. With the Reds, Power established himself as a major league pitcher, becoming first the team's closer and later a dependable starter. This doesn't mean that the Dodgers didn't teach Power anything. Under the tutelage of wild men Jay Johnstone, Terry Forster, Jerry Reuss, and Don Stanhouse, Power learned plenty about the fine art of prankstership.

For example, Power was witness to a prank Johnstone and friends pulled on Dodgers manager Tommy Lasorda in spring training at the Dodgers' famous Vero Beach complex.

"I was two doors down from Lasorda in the complex," says Power. "One night when Tommy was out for dinner, they broke into his room and removed the mouthpiece out of his phone, so he could hear the person on the other end but the person on the other end wouldn't be able to hear him. After Lasorda came back and went to bed, they tied his door handle with a ski rope to a palm tree. The next morning when he got up and tried to leave his room he couldn't open the door. He looked out the window, saw the rope, and said, 'Ha, ha, very funny.' He got on the phone and called the front desk. He heard the woman say hello, so he said, 'They've tied my door shut and I can't get out. Send somebody down to cut the rope and let me out.' But of course the woman at the desk couldn't hear him. She kept saying, 'Hello . . . Mr. Lasorda? . . . Hello?'

"By this time I was awake, because he was screaming bloody murder and cussing. I was watching him from my room, but I wasn't about to help him. He tried the phone again but slammed it down. Then he tried to pull on his door again, but he could only open it about an inch because those guys had stretched that rope tight! Finally, he had no choice but to resort to the most degrading thing for a major league manager to do in the situation: he tried to crawl out of his window. He opened the window, knocked the screen off, and started to climb out. The window only partially opened, though, so he got stuck. He was half out and half in. So there he was, Tommy Lasorda, manager of the Los Angeles Dodgers, bright red in the face, screaming bloody murder for somebody to come help him get out of there. It so happened that a few minutes later a delivery guy came by, and he helped Tommy get out."

Power played a more active role in another prank that occurred years later, toward the end of his career, when he was an important member of the Cleveland Indians' bullpen. "We were playing the Angels in Anaheim," says Power, "and there were five of us relievers, sitting way out in the bullpen, bored to death. There were hardly any people in the stands near us at all. We were sitting with our feet up against the gate, trying to figure out something to do to break up the monotony, when a rat scurried into the bullpen from the outfield and ran right under our feet. We started chasing it all over the bullpen—there was dust flying everywhere—but we couldn't catch it, and it ran under a tarp that had been folded over several times and laid to the side. Eric Plunk stepped on the tarp and killed the rat. He said he wasn't trying to kill it; he was just trying to hold it in place so we could catch it. I don't know what we would have done with it had we caught it alive.

"Anyway, now we had a dead rat in the bullpen. We tried to think of something to do with it, but we couldn't come up with anything. After a while, Steve Olin said, 'Hey, I know. Let's light it on fire!'

"So we did. We got some string and hung it from the top of the fence, and then somebody put a match to that thing. The whole thing burned, not just the fur but the whole rat, and it smelled awful, just terrible! People in the stands smelled it, so they started coming over to the bullpen with these pained looks on their faces: 'What is that horrible smell?'

"When the rat quit burning, I got it into a plastic bag and tied the bag up. With the bag tied up you couldn't smell it anymore. Then we thought, 'Now we've got something really smelly, really disgusting! Now what can we do with it?'

"The day before, a bunch of guys had gone out to the Nike factory and gotten some new stuff. Rick Adair, our pitching coach, had gone along and had gotten a brand-new pair of turf shoes, and he'd been bragging about them: 'Yeah, if you want to wear my new shoes, you can ask, but I doubt if I'll let you wear 'em, because they're brand-new.' And he kept making a big deal about them being Nikes because all of us guys in the bullpen wore Reeboks. You know, stuff like that. So I said, 'I know what we can do with this rat.'

"After the game, we took the rat into the clubhouse. It was still in that plastic bag, so it didn't smell. We waited for everybody else to leave, and then we reached down into Rick's locker and pulled those Nikes out. They were still in the box and hadn't even been laced up yet. We took the packing out of one of the shoes, opened the bag, slid that rat into the shoe, put the lid back on the box, and put the box right back into Rick's locker.

"Now, I can't describe the smell of that clubhouse the next day. I don't know what a dead person smells like, but this was the worst smell I'd ever smelled in my life. The clubhouse guys were going crazy. They kept saying, 'Something died in here, but we can't find it.' They couldn't find it, but they had determined that it was somewhere over by the coaches' lockers. All the bullpen got there early, because we couldn't wait for Adair to come in. Finally, he walked in, and right away, in that North Carolina twang of his, he said, 'Geezus Kriiist, what's that smell!?'

"We were already having a hard time keeping a straight face, but we agreed with him—'Yeah. Man, that's awful'—and played dumb. We watched him as he went over and sat down in front of his locker. He started looking over the pitching reports, but he just couldn't concentrate on them. He kept saying, 'Gol-all-lee, it's worse over here than anywhere else. . . . I think it's behind my locker.' Now, all this time we were busting up inside, but we turned away from Rick, put our arms over our faces, stepped inside the trainer's room for a minute, so he couldn't see us laughing. Finally, we saw him reach into his locker and pull out that brand-new Nike box. He knew it then. He put the box on the floor a couple of feet away, stretched his leg out, and flipped off the lid of the box with his toe. The very next word out of his mouth was 'POWER!' And then he added, 'I'll kill you!'

"He knew right away that it was the bullpen that had done it, and he knew right away also that it was probably me who had instigated it.

"Rick put the lid back on the box and then dropped the whole thing, those brand-new Nikes, right in the trash. And of course the clubhouse boys got it out of there as fast as they could. They opened all the doors and had fans blowing in some fresh air. Still, everybody who came in that night said, 'Whew! What's that awful smell?' "

Nothing, not even baseball, is all fun and games, and in 1993 the Indians suffered one of the worst tragedies in baseball history when two of their pitchers (Steve Olin and Tim Crews) died and a third pitcher (Bob Ojeda) was seriously injured in a boating accident during spring training. The accident occurred when Crews's eighteen-foot, open-air fishing boat crashed into a dock on Little Lake Nellie in Clermont, Florida, near the Indians' spring training home in Winter Haven. The tragedy profoundly affected Power, who had planned to join his teammates for their off-day outing but changed his mind for inexplicable reasons.

"A day off in spring training," says Power, "is extremely rare, but Cleveland had scheduled one, and we were really looking forward to it. I had made plans to go out to the lake with Steve Olin and Tim Crews and their families to barbecue, fish, ride horses, and go boating. I grew up in Oklahoma and Kansas, and all of those things had been big parts of my childhood. So this was a slam dunk, something I could hardly wait to do.

"But then I woke up the morning of our day off, and I knew instantly that I wasn't going to go. I didn't know why . . . I had no idea why I wasn't going to go, but I could not convince myself to get in the car and drive out to the lake. I didn't have a headache or a stomachache. Physically, I felt perfectly fine. And all day long I kept telling myself, 'You should still go. You've got time. They're going to be out there all day.' But I could not convince myself to go out there and join this day of doing everything I loved to do. I wound up spending the day running errands and doing all kinds of chores I would normally not do in a million years.

"At dusk, which turned out to be about the time of the accident, I went out to get something to eat. A couple of hours later, when I got back, my phone was ringing. It was my mother calling from Kansas. The newspeople had interrupted the ball game on TV that night to say that three Cleveland Indians pitchers had been in a terrible boating accident—two killed, one seriously injured, no names. Well, my parents, knowing me, just knew that I would have been out there on that lake, boating and fishing. When I said hello, all my mother said was 'Thank God.'

"'What's up, Mom?' I said. From the sound of her voice I knew something was wrong. I was thinking maybe something had happened to my dad or one of my sisters out in Kansas.

"'You mean you haven't heard yet?' she said.

"And then I said, 'What is wrong? You're scaring me to death.' At this point I was starting to wonder if something had happened to my wife Karen or one of our kids. Finally, she told me what had happened. I got off the phone with her and called my wife. Karen had also heard about the accident, but she also knew who had been involved in it. Needless to say, I was just devastated. I had grown close to Tim Crews that spring because we were similar-type pitchers and also because he was an old Dodger like me, and we loved trading stories about the Dodgers. I was even closer to Steve Olin, who had become like a brother to me. Actually, that whole bullpen from the year before was very close, because we all had an all-for-one, one-for-all attitude that is pretty rare today. We had five very unselfish guys trying to do a job as one, as a unit, and we didn't care if Steve got the save, if Derek Lilliquist got the save, or if I got it or Eric Plunk or Kevin Wickander. We were happy for whichever guy got the save, and we were really happy for our group. We had a saying, in fact, which illustrated the closeness we felt: 'Screw the starters. Give all the wins to the bullpen.'

"It wasn't until the shock had worn off and I'd had time to grieve and lose control and then regain control that I came to the same realization that most blessed people come to: that God is in control of our lives. For me, acknowledging that fact was like putting on a suit of clothes or a second skin that never comes off. And I said, 'Okay, Lord, I know You are there, I know you are in control, and whatever you have in mind for me to do with the rest of my life, I'm up for it, because I know You just saved my life!'

"At this point I started looking backward at my life and I was able to recall a number of close calls throughout my life, times when I'd been a few minutes or a few feet away from some disaster or even death. And I realized that my whole life, without my having asked, Jesus Christ had already been my Lord and Savior and that, furthermore, He was willing to be the same thing for everybody else. When that hit me it was like a building falling on me. 'You've got to be kidding me,' I thought. 'These things in the Bible are all true. They're not some stories that somebody just made up.' And that's when I really refocused my life. I wouldn't say that the accident completely changed my life, because I hadn't been a terrible, terrible person before that, but it helped me put the focus of my life on what really matters, which is my relationship to Christ."

Professional sports in America produce far too many pampered, irresponsible players who, upon retirement, have trouble becoming productive members of society. But don't include in that group Ted Power, who for the past several years has worked as an administrator for Christian Sports International, the Pittsburgh-based organization that attempts to introduce the message of Jesus Christ to young people through clinics in a variety of sports.

PEDRO RAMOS

For four straight years Pedro Ramos led American League pitchers in losses. Pitching for the Washington Senators and the expansion Minnesota Twins, Ramos lost 18 (1958), 19 (1959), 18 (1960), and 20 games (1961). Despite this dismal record, many observers thought that Ramos could be a decent pitcher, and Ramos later proved it. Acquired by the New York Yankees in early September, Ramos shored up the Yankees' bullpen and helped the Bronx Bombers prevail in the tough 1964 pennant race; appearing in 13 games, Pedro fashioned a 1.25 ERA while winning 1 game and saving another 8. The following year Ramos became the Yankees' first-line closer, saving 19 games in 1965 and 13 in 1966.

Pedro had pretty good pop in his bat for a pitcher—he hit 15 home runs in his career—and he was fast enough afoot that managers often used him as a pinch runner. The eccentric Ramos claimed he was the fastest runner in the major leagues, and he repeatedly challenged Mickey Mantle to a race to prove his claim, but Mantle never deigned to accept Pedro's challenge.

Not surprisingly, Ramos was just as notorious for his off-the-field antics. Pitcher Sonny Siebert remembers the worst day Ramos ever had, at the ballpark or away from it.

"This happened in 1964 when Pedro and I were with the Cleveland Indians," says Siebert. "Now, first of all, you have to know that Pedro loved to dress like a cowboy. He'd wear cowboy boots and a cowboy hat and a belt with holsters and guns on both sides. We called him the 'Cuban Cowboy.'

"The second thing you need to know is that Pedro had married a beautiful girl. In fact, she was a former Miss Cuba. Well, one day Pedro was lying on the bed watching TV, and he asked his wife to turn it off. She didn't move fast enough to suit him, so Pedro pulled out his pistols and started shooting the TV: blam! blam! blam!

"He destroyed his TV set, lost his wife, who divorced him, and got evicted from his apartment . . . all in one motion. So after that, we started calling him 'Pistol Pete.' "

POKEY REESE

Opening Day of the baseball season is a big deal everywhere, but in Cincinnati it is huge. There's a big parade downtown, the Reds' ballpark is decked out as if it were hosting a World Series game, and kids and adults alike play hooky in order to attend the game. Cincinnati's 1998 opener against the San Diego Padres had an especially authentic circuslike atmosphere due to the menagerie of animals on hand at Cinergy Field. Before the game the Reds released doves and pigeons, and horse-drawn carriages paraded around the field. Reds owner Marge Schott took her Saint Bernard onto the field and asked her players if any of them wanted the dog to lick their faces for good luck. Bigger—er, more huge—yet, an elephant and two camels left over from the parade trod the AstroTurf as part of the pregame festivities. The Reds thought of everything to make the pregame celebration perfect, including keeping the playing field unsoiled by having a Cincinnati Zoo employee follow behind the elephant while carrying a garbage bag. As the elephant catcher, having completed his task without error, walked off the field minutes before the start of the game, he raised his arms in triumph, and the crowd roared its approval.

It was, unfortunately, nearly the last thing Reds fans had to cheer about all day. After six and a half innings the Reds trailed 10–0 and wound up losing 10–2. It was a disappointing, if not totally unexpected, outcome, given the Reds' young and inexperienced lineup, weakened by the absence of veteran shortstop Barry Larkin, who sat out with an injury.

What was totally unexpected was the erratic play of Larkin's replacement, Calvin "Pokey" Reese, who helped bury the Reds early by making four errors in the first three innings. Reese overthrew first base in a double-play attempt in the first inning, bobbled a grounder to begin the third, booted another grounder later in the same inning, and then kicked the ball trying to retrieve it, which allowed a Padres runner to advance an extra base. It was a nightmarish day for Reese, who had earned a reputation as an excellent-fielding shortstop while filling in for the ailing Larkin much of the previous summer.

Reds pitcher Mike Remlinger was pretty understanding after being victimized by Pokey's shoddy glovework. "Pokey won't make four errors in a game the rest of his career. I'll bet you any amount of money on that," he said. Reds manager Jack McKeon also downplayed the importance of the errors, joking with Reese after the dismal third inning: "Why don't you boot a couple more and go for the record?"

As for Reese, he too realized it was just one of those days, but he felt bad about it nevertheless. Asked to comment after the game about the man who followed behind the elephant with a garbage bag, he said, "I wouldn't want that job. Of course, if I make four errors again, maybe they'll make me do that job."

PETE ROSE

Pete Rose may have some rough edges, but it is a mistake to confuse them with a lack of intelligence. For example, a smug reporter who once asked Rose if he'd ever gone to college received a reply that put him neatly in his place.

"No, I've never gone to college," said Rose, "but I've thought about buying one."

Rose may never have obtained a college degree, but no one ever displayed more genius than he on a baseball diamond. Former pitcher Ted Power is certainly impressed with Rose's baseball IQ.

"It was a real joy playing with Pete Rose," says Power, "because of all the men I met in baseball, he understood better than anyone else how to pick out an opponent's weakness and use it to his advantage like he'd known about it for years. Pete could pick out something before a game, and if he had a chance to use it during the game, he would use it. Other guys might notice something—maybe a pitcher tipping off his curveball by pointing up the index finger of his glove hand—but when it actually comes down to seeing it, reacting to it, and taking advantage of it, they can't do it. They just can't do it. But Pete could do it. In fact, those were the moments he lived for.

"I remember one time Pete was sitting on the bench in our dugout watching the other team take infield. Pete and I were the only ones in the dugout. Everybody else was back in the clubhouse. And I asked him what the heck he was doing, because nobody ever makes it a point to watch the other team take infield. They might watch batting practice or the starting pitcher warm up, but not infield. He said, 'Watch this right fielder. Every time he catches a ball on the ground, he keeps his head down and looks the ball into his hand and then he raises his head up to throw. If I hit a single to right today, I'm going to be standing on second base, and I won't even have to slide.'

"I laughed and said something like 'Yeah, sure, you old fart. Try that and you'll get your ass thrown out by a mile and be embarrassed.' I thought that, see, because by that time Pete wasn't a spring chicken anymore.

" 'You watch,' he said.

"Well, about the sixth inning, he hit a grounder between first and second. The right fielder came in to play it and put his head down as he pulled the ball into his glove. Pete charged down to first the way he always did, but instead of rounding the bag and pulling up, he hit the bag going full speed and kept right on going for second. When the right fielder looked up and saw Pete heading for second, he panicked and bobbled the ball. Pete pulled into second standing up, and when he turned around he had that big stupid grin of his on his face. He looked into our dugout right at me, as if to say, 'See, see . . . I told you so!' He was just amazing."

BABE RUTH

B abe Ruth is truly immortal. Of all the baseball greats past and present, Ruth is the one whose exploits are most famous and whose visage is most recognizable. Not that the Babe needs any help, but Willis "Buster" Gardner does his best each summer to keep the Babe's memory alive by arranging for the Babe to walk about the streets of Cooperstown, New York, during Induction Weekend. Each year thousands of baseball fans on the crowded streets of Cooperstown are startled and delighted to see the Babe, in the flesh and wearing his old-fashioned Yankees cap and pin-striped jersey, freely signing autographs and posing for pictures.

Of course, it's not the Babe back from the dead who walks the streets of Cooperstown but Gardner himself, who bears an uncanny facial and physical resemblance to Ruth. The gregarious, paunchy Gardner is so convincing as the Babe that he makes paid appearances around the country. He regularly stars at National Babe Ruth League Tournaments, and in 1998 he was hired by the New York Mets to appear at all three games of the Mets-Yankees first interleague "Subway Series." In fact, as Gardner proudly points out, Mets owner Nelson Doubleday called him personally to ask him to make the appearance.

According to Gardner, his Ruth impersonation started about ten years ago when his daughter Rita looked carefully at a Babe Ruth photograph, compared it to her father, and said, "Dad, this is you!"

"At first, I shrugged it off," says Gardner, "but Rita persisted. She bought me an old-style Yankees cap, and I had to admit that wearing it really brought out the resemblance. When we added the jersey with Babe's number 3 on it, things really started taking off.

"I normally get paid for my appearances, but I come up here to Cooperstown for free because the Hall of Famers enjoy seeing me as much as anybody else. I've come up from my home in Oberlin, Ohio, for the past seven inductions, and every year on Friday when the returning Hall of Famers start coming into town, the first person they ask about is me: 'Where's the Babe? Where's he at?' I know every one of the Hall of Famers, and it's nice to be able to rub elbows with them, but I also get a kick out of mixing with the fans. On Saturday and Sunday when the streets are packed with people, so many fans want a picture or an autograph that it takes me an hour and a half to walk two blocks down Main Street."

Gardner's resemblance to the Babe is so dramatic that it makes one wonder if he is not actually related to the Ruth family. "No, there is no relationship, at least none that I'm aware of," says Gardner. Still, at times and in certain places, the resemblance can be downright spooky. "About three years ago I was visiting the Hall of Fame Museum," says Gardner, "and I went into the large room that houses the permanent Babe Ruth exhibit. There was only one other guy in the room, and he was looking at something in one of the display cases on the wall. I walked up and stood behind him, looking over his shoulder. When he turned around and saw me, wearing my Yankees cap and jersey, it scared him half to death. 'Wh-what are you doing here?' he asked. 'Oh, I just thought I'd check in to see what they've done to my room lately,' I said. He said, 'Oh, my God!' and practically ran out of the room, presumably to go tell somebody connected with the Hall of Fame that he'd just seen Babe Ruth's ghost in the Museum."

CHRIS SABO

No one heralded Chris Sabo's arrival in the big leagues in 1988, but Cincinnati Reds fans approved of the over-achieving third baseman from the very first moment he wad-dled bowleggedly onto the turf of Riverfront Stadium. In Sabo, who looked and acted like a regular guy from the neighborhood, the fans had somebody they could identify with. The ever-hustling Sabo was modest, appreciative, and so unostentatious that he continued to drive a beat-up Ford Escort long after the major league code of conspicuous consumption dictated that he own only vehicles the average American could never afford. Moreover, with his old-fashioned burr haircut and protective goggles, Sabo hardly looked like a celebrity, even though his teammates collared him with the nickname "Spuds" because they thought he resembled the star of a series of beer commer-cials, a ring-eyed dog named Spuds McKenzie.

Although a lot of the so-called experts never seemed to be impressed with him, Sabo also showed he could play a little bit. He won the National League Rookie of the Year Award in 1988, made the NL All-Star team in 1988, '90, and '91, and starred in the 1990 World Series, batting .563 with two home runs. After the Reds swept the highly favored Oakland A's in that Series, Sabo delivered what for him was a sharp rebuke to his critics: "A number of publications put me down before this season. One publication said I wouldn't make the Reds' club this year. Well, all those publications can . . . they can jump off a bridge."

Sabo pretty much conducted himself like a Boy Scout throughout his career, but he did become embroiled in one controversy, even if it did come about accidentally.

On July 29, 1996, Sabo led off the second inning for the Reds in a game against the Houston Astros at Riverfront Stadium in Cincinnati. Fouling off a pitch from left-hander Mike Hampton, Sabo cracked his bat. The Reds' batboy brought out three bats that Sabo had scavenged from a pile of discarded pitchers' batting-practice bats, and Sabo chose one of them as a replacement. He immediately cracked that bat, too, on another foul ball, but this time he decided to continue with the cracked bat, not wanting to risk breaking three bats during a single plate appearance. Sabo made a little better contact on his third swing, but the bat shattered and produced only a weak pop-up to shortstop Orlando Miller. While Miller had to keep his eyes on the baseball, everyone else in the ballpark was focused on something else: the five or six pieces of cork that were fluttering around the infield, evidence that the bat Sabo had used had been illegally tampered with. (Although there is no evidence that corking works, many players believe that using a corked bat— a bat with a barrel filled with cork, sawdust, Styrofoam, or some other substance lighter than wood—enables them to hit a ball as much as fifty feet farther than they can hit it using a regulation bat.)

Players on both teams laughed at the spectacle, but umpire crew chief Ed Montague immediately threw Sabo out of the game. Sabo's protest that "it wasn't my bat" fell on deaf ears, but Montague later said that he had a tendency to believe Sabo because he noticed that Sabo had grabbed the doctored replacement bat at random from the batboy. After the game Sabo used a rhetorical question as evidence of his innocence: "Do you think I'd be dumb enough to stay up there with a cracked bat if I knew it was corked?" He also clearly stated that "I've never corked a bat, and I've never had one corked for me."

Despite Sabo's logic and believable protestations of innocence, the National League suspended him for seven games and fined the Reds $25,000. Cincinnati general manager Jim Bowden didn't blame Sabo for the incident, but he reacted strongly to it. "I don't think it's funny," he said, "and I didn't appreciate our players laughing about it. The Reds don't condone corked bats. It's an embarrassment to the Reds. It questions the integrity of baseball and the Reds. We are ashamed of it." Bowden also promised that the club would x-ray all the players' bats, including the pitchers' batting-practice bats, to ensure that a repeat of the incident never occurred.

The best perspective on the incident came from Reds catcher Eddie Taubensee, who focused on the outcome of Sabo's at bat. "Does this mean that if the bat Chris used hadn't been corked, he would have popped to the pitcher [instead of to the shortstop]?"

MARGE SCHOTT

Baseball is the most beautiful of games, but it is also a business. At times, and especially when tough personnel decisions must be made, it can be a cold, impersonal business. Every player who has been released, sold, or traded knows the feeling well. However, as former Cincinnati Reds pitcher Ted Power knows, compassion sometimes comes to bat when you least expect it.

"At the beginning of the 1983 season, which was my first year with the Reds after I had been traded from the Dodgers, there was a party for the team at owner Marge Schott's house. We were there for an outdoor barbecue on the grounds of her estate, and it was a very warm day. At that point I didn't really know anybody, not even Marge, so I felt that I was there to get something to eat and to get to know my new teammates.

"I finished off a plate of food and a beer, and as I walked over to the bar to get another beer, I noticed a dog that needed some attention. Because of the barbecue the party had a Western theme, complete with an Old West–type covered wagon. This dog had wrapped its chain around one of the wagon wheels, and so it couldn't move out of the sun. Its tongue was hanging out, and it was obviously hot and thirsty.

"I unwound the dog's chain from the wagon wheel, chained the dog under a tree so it could lie in the shade, and filled up its bowl with some fresh water.

"I thought the dog belonged to a ballplayer, but it was Schottzie, Marge's dog, and, as I found out later, she saw the whole thing. After I had taken care of the dog, Marge pointed

DON POLLARD

at me and asked somebody, 'Who's that tall fella over there?' The reply, of course, was that I was the team's new pitcher from the Dodgers. Marge said, 'He seems like a nice young man.'

"Four years later the Reds were working up a trade with the Yankees. The Reds wanted a left-handed pitcher, and they did wind up getting one, Dennis Rasmussen, from New York. When general manager Bill Bergesh went into Marge's office to go over the trade with her, my name was number one at the top of the list of players to be traded. Marge said, 'Take his name off the list.' Although what I had done was really no big deal, Marge never forgot the way I had treated her dog. She also said to Bergesh, 'Besides, don't you know Power and his wife just moved into a new house here in Cincinnati, and they're expecting their second child?' Marge simply wouldn't listen to the baseball reasons her people had for thinking I was the one who should be traded, and so it was Bill Gullickson who went to the Yankees, not me. So, you see, Marge has done things and has said things that I wouldn't have judged to be the right things to do or say, but I know that she does have a heart."

DON POLLARD

SEINFELD

The airing of the final episode of *Seinfeld* on May 14, 1998, was a major moment in the history of American television, and given the show's extensive use of baseball personalities and plots, it was a stroke of marketing genius for the Double-A Knoxville (Tennessee) Smokies to hold a *Seinfeld* characters look-alike contest as a promotion.

According to the Smokies' director of marketing and sales, Mark Seaman, Jeff Shoaf (the director of group sales) not only came up with the idea for the contest but also discovered the contest's eventual winner in the crowd. "We decided that we needed five judges for the contest," says Seaman. "We asked a couple of season-ticket holders that we knew to do it, and we went into the stands to recruit three more people at random. That's when Jeff saw this guy who is a dead ringer for Jerry Seinfeld. Jeff said, 'You're gonna be in the contest, right?' It hadn't even occurred to the guy to enter.

"As it turned out, we had a total of five entries. There was one George, one Elaine, one Kramer, and two Jerrys. We took them out onto the field in the middle of the third inning for the judging, and we said something like 'This is Joe Smith as George . . . this is Mary Jones as Elaine,' and so on. Then we took them back out in the middle of the seventh to announce the winners. We had a third-prize winner, a second-prize winner, and a grand-prize winner. It wasn't even close. The Jerry look-alike that Jeff picked out in the stands won hands down. The guy who was supposed to resemble Kramer looked nothing like him. He wet his hair to make it stand up like Kramer's, but that was about it. The George look-alike wasn't even close, nor was the Elaine look-alike, although she was holding a bottle of water as a prop to imitate the way Elaine is always drinking bottled water on the show.

"The guy who won is named Chris Robinson, and he won some pretty good prizes: two airplane tickets to New York City, a two-night stay in a nice hotel, and two pairs of tickets to both a Yankees game and the Kramer Reality Tour. He was pretty calm about winning the contest. All he did was kind of wave a little bit to the crowd. I think he was a little shocked about the whole thing. The funny thing is that he wound up entering and winning another Seinfeld look-alike contest held later that week by our local NBC affiliate, WBIR.

"With such great prizes on the line, you would have thought that more people would have entered the contest, just to have a shot at winning them. We thought there would at least have been numerous George look-alikes entered. I mean, how many millions of short, pudgy, balding men with glasses are there out there? Despite only five entries, we felt the promotion was a great success because we got a lot of publicity from it.

"How would the promotion have turned out had George Costanza been in charge of it? Well, George probably would have tried to rig the contest so that he could have won it himself, but whatever he would have done, it would have been a disaster, that's for sure!"

NORM SHERRY

Pitching coaches have to know pitching: grips, deliveries, release points, etc. But it's not always being able to pass on technical knowledge that makes a pitching coach valuable to a pitcher trying to work his way out of a jam.

Ex–Giants pitcher Mike Krukow once found himself in a tight spot early in the first game of a doubleheader against the Montreal Expos before a packed house at Montreal's Olympic Stadium. With runners on first and third, one out, and the Expos' big bats coming up to the plate, Giants manager Roger Craig sent his pitching coach, Norm Sherry, out to talk to Krukow. Wearing turf shoes, Sherry jogged jauntily across the AstroTurf of Olympic Stadium with his head down, as was his custom. When he neared the mound and the conference of Giants infielders gathered around Krukow, Sherry tripped over the cutout where the AstroTurf ends and the dirt of the mound begins. He fell flat across the pitching mound, his head landing at Krukow's feet.

Sherry picked himself up, brushed the dirt off his face, pants, and shirt, and asked Krukow in all seriousness, without cracking a smile, "Do you think anybody saw that?" Without saying another word, Sherry turned around and trotted back to the dugout.

"I was laughing so hard, I could barely throw," says Krukow. Loosened up by Sherry's slapstick routine, Krukow threw a great sinker on his next pitch to the dangerous Andre Dawson, who promptly hit a ground ball to short that the Giants turned into a double play to end the inning.

ERIC SHOW

Eric Show (rhymes with "how") will always be best remembered for being the pitcher who gave up Pete Rose's record-setting 4,192nd hit and then sat down on the pitching mound when he felt that the standing ovation Rose received was taking too long. Show's teammates on the San Diego Padres remember him for other reasons. For one thing, Show was the workhorse of the San Diego pitching staff; he led the Padres in innings pitched five out of the six seasons between 1983 and 1988. For another, he was a very unique individual whose entire world was not consumed by balls and strikes.

As Gene Walter, another former Padres pitcher, says, "Eric Show was on a different level from everybody else. He was an extremely talented person in a lot of ways. He had been a physics major in college, and he was an accomplished jazz guitar player. He was so good that we'd walk into the Grand Hyatt Hotel in New York City, and there would be Eric playing guitar with the band that was working at the hotel.

"I'll never forget the night I learned just how much music meant to Eric. This happened during my rookie year, 1985. I had pitched the night before, so I was planning to relax and to watch the game from the bullpen; however, Dick Williams called on the bullpen phone and invited me to sit in the dugout. If the skipper invites you to sit in the dugout, you sit in the dugout, especially if you're a rookie, so I walked down to the dugout and sat about ten feet away from Dick.

"At some point in the game Eric was at the plate, and he was trying to bunt. Now, Eric liked to hit and took more batting practice than some of our hitters. And in fact he was a pretty good hitter. The year before, he had hit .246 with three home runs. Nevertheless, he couldn't get the bunt down. He struck out trying to bunt and looked downright silly doing it. When he came back into the dugout, he sat down on my left and said, 'Man, I was up half the night trying to compose a new song, but I couldn't work out the ending. Just as I was squaring around to bunt, the music started to come to me. I was going "doo-doo dah, doo-doo-doo dah," and it messed me up bunting.'

"I didn't say anything, but I winced and thought, 'Geez, I hope Dick Williams didn't hear that,' because he would have gone stark raving mad if he'd known one of his ballplayers didn't get a bunt down because he was preoccupied with composing music at the plate!"

SONNY SIEBERT

Sonny Siebert (1964–75), who pitched for the Indians, Red Sox, Rangers, Cardinals, Padres, and A's, credits his success in the big leagues to an outstanding curveball and his willingness to pitch inside. Now the pitching coach for the Triple-A Colorado Sky Sox, Siebert teaches his charges that that same willingness to pitch inside, to brush hitters back off the plate, is the key to their own pitching success and advancement to the big leagues. Here are some of the war stories Siebert tells to illustrate the efficaciousness of his philosophy.

"I guess the best proof that I was never afraid to pitch inside is the fact that I intentionally hit the first batter I ever faced in the big leagues with the very first pitch I ever threw in a major league game," says Siebert. "And not only that, the batter was Mickey Mantle.

"Here's how it happened. The Yankees came into Cleveland that year for a four-game series, with single games on Friday and Saturday and a doubleheader on Sunday. The Yankees might not have been quite as good as in previous years, but with Mantle and Maris and guys like Elston Howard, Joe Pepitone, and Tom Tresh, they still had plenty of mashers. They blew us out on Friday and Saturday, and we used every available pitcher except for Sunday's scheduled starters and me. I called my wife Saturday night and said, 'I'm gone. They're going to send me down to the minors.'

"Dick Donovan started the second game on Sunday for us, and the Yankees scored seven runs in the first two innings. Then, for some reason, the Yankees knocked down Rocky Colavito, our best hitter. This really pissed off our manager, George Strickland. George called on the bullpen phone, and I thought, 'There's no way they're going to pitch me,' but George ordered me to warm up. When I went out to pitch the top of the third, George told me to hit one of their first two batters in retaliation. 'Mantle or Maris, take your pick,' he said. I didn't see any point in wasting time, so I hit Mantle in the ribs with my first pitch in the big leagues.

"Mantle didn't say anything to me, but he did look over at Strickland in our dugout, because he knew George had ordered me to hit him. I went six innings and struck out eleven, and that game secured my spot on the roster. I had been competing with two other pitchers, but after that game the club sent them back to the minors, not me. More significantly, Mickey Mantle couldn't touch me after that."

"I also knocked down Carl Yastrzemski one day . . . in batting practice!" Siebert recalls. "Here's how that came about. Right after the start of the 1969 season I got traded from Cleveland to Boston. A rookie named Mike Garman was throwing batting practice to Tony Conigliaro, Yastrzemski, and Reggie Smith. Garman was having a little trouble with his control, so Conigliaro stepped out of the box and said, 'Throw the f**king ball over the plate, rookie.' Mike was embarrassed and he started trying harder, which only made it more difficult for him to throw strikes.

"After he finished pitching to his group, Mike complained about Conigliaro and asked me what he should do if the same thing happened again. 'You should knock 'em down. Get some respect,' I said.

"'That's Tony C.! I can't do that,' he said.

"'Well, that's what you should have done, and that's what I'd do,' I said.

"The next day I was throwing some bp. Now, the way I looked at it, bp was really just as much pitching practice for me as it was batting practice for the hitters. I'd throw the first five or six pitches to each batter right down the middle, but then I'd start moving the ball around and pitch to different spots. That's what I did when Yaz was batting, and just like Conigliaro had done the day before, Yaz backed off the plate and yelled, 'Throw the f**king ball over the plate!' Yaz dug back in, and I knocked him down with the very next pitch.

"He didn't say a word, just walked out of the cage, picked up his glove, and started walking out to the outfield. I ran over to him and said, 'Hey, let's get this straightened out right now. If you're gonna show me up like that, there's gonna be trouble.'

"'I didn't mean anything by that, Siebs,' he said. I told him how I approached bp, and he said he didn't have a problem with it. Later on that night, right before I told my wife what had happened, I said, 'Pack up, I'm going to be traded,' but I wasn't. In fact, everything worked out well. Before I knocked him down, Yaz acted like he was above the pitchers, but I got him to respect me, and we even became good friends."

"And then there was the time I had to knock down Danny Cater, who used to be my best friend," Siebert says. "Danny and I had gotten close playing winter ball together in Puerto Rico. Back in the States he started hitting me pretty good. It seems like he was always going two-for-three or three-for-four against me. My wife, who was baseball smart, asked me about it. 'Why does he hit you so well? Is it because he's your friend and you don't want to pitch him tight and risk hitting him?' That woke me up, and I realized she was exactly right.

"Now, Cater was the kind of guy who liked to be on the field early, and he liked to socialize. He was always talking to you. The next time we played against each other and I was scheduled to pitch, he did his usual thing: 'How's Carol? How are the kids?' I didn't answer him, so he asked me what was wrong. 'Hey, Danny, be alive tonight,' I said.

" 'What? You gonna hit me? What are you talking about?' he said.

" 'Just be loose in there tonight,' I said.

"The first time he came up I threw the first pitch under his chin. But he was ready for it, and he got out of the way without any trouble. I thought, 'That didn't really serve my purpose,' so I threw another knockdown on the very next pitch. It was the best knockdown I've ever seen. It scared him to death, and he pitched himself backward and down to the ground as if his life literally depended on it.

"Danny has never spoken to me since. I lost a friend, but I gained an edge on a hitter who used to own me. In fact, I don't think Cater ever got a hit off me again. It taught me that it's tough for a pitcher to be friends with a hitter, because to be successful you simply must use both sides of the plate."

MAYO SMITH

Mayo Smith made one of the boldest moves in World Series history in 1968 when he replaced weak-hitting Ray Oyler at shortstop with outfielder Mickey Stanley. The move not only did not hurt the Tigers defensively, as Stanley performed well at short, but it also allowed Smith to maximize the Tigers' offensive punch by keeping all three of his other outfielders, Willie Horton, Jim Northrup, and Al Kaline, in the lineup. Despite this success, which played a big part in the Tigers' seven-game victory over the St. Louis Cardinals, many of the Detroit players did not think very highly of Smith's managerial abilities. In fact, according to pitcher Jon Warden, the Tigers routinely overcame what they considered to be Smith's bad managing during the regular season by ignoring his ill-advised orders while pretending to follow them. On occasion, though, it was impossible to even pretend to follow Mayo's orders.

"One night our pitcher found himself in a jam, so Mayo got on the dugout phone and called the bullpen," says Warden.

"I answered the phone and heard Mayo's gravelly voice say, 'Get Timmerman up.'

"I paused for a second, then I said, 'Timmerman ain't here.'

" 'Well, by God, where's he at?'

" 'Hell, Mayo, you sent him down to Toledo two days ago.'

" 'Oh, yeah. Well, get Dobson up, then.'

"That was Mayo, trying to warm up a pitcher who wasn't even on the team any longer."

TRACY STALLARD

On the last day of the 1961 American League season, October 31, rookie right-hander Tracy Stallard of the Boston Red Sox started against the New York Yankees at Yankee Stadium in front of only 23,154 fans. This was a paltry attendance figure, given the fact that the game would be Roger Maris's last chance to break Babe Ruth's hallowed record for most home runs (60) in a single season.

In the fourth inning with no score in the game, one out, and nobody on base, Stallard faced Maris for the second time that day. The gutsy Stallard missed with his first two pitches, but then threw "my best fastball" over the plate. Maris hit the pitch into the right-field seats for his sixty-first homer of the season and, as it turned out, the only run of the ball game. The home run made both Maris and Stallard famous. Today, the good-natured Stallard is one of the most popular former ballplayers on the old-timers' golf outing and fantasy camp circuit, and his peers enjoy kidding him about his role in the historic Maris-Ruth drama. "Hey, Tracy," they ask, "if McGwire or Griffey gets to sixty-one home runs, are you coming out of retirement to serve up number sixty-two?"

Stallard pitched in two other historic games, for the infant New York Mets, to whom he was traded in December 1962. On May 31, 1964, Stallard took the loss against the San Francisco Giants as the two clubs played a 7-hour, 23-minute marathon, the longest game in major league history. Less than a month later, June 21, he found himself on the wrong end of a perfect game that Philadelphia's Jim Bunning threw against the Mets.

Altogether, Stallard lost twenty games for the hapless Mets that year to lead the National League in losses. "I've thought about it," says Tracy, "and there ain't no one else but me to blame for every one of them losses." Nice try, Tracy, but having pitched for a team full of Bonehead Merkles had a lot to do with your rotten record. After all, in five of those losses the Mets were shut out, and other games were given away by teammates as freely as one-size-fits-all caps on Cap Day. In the second game of the season, for instance, Stallard battled Jim Bunning to a 1–1 tie after seven innings in Philadelphia. The Phillies' Bobby Wine doubled to open the bottom of the eighth, but he retired the next two batters. He then induced the dangerous Dick Allen to hit a routine grounder to second baseman Amado Samuel, which would have ended the inning except that first baseman Tim Harkness dropped Samuel's throw. Tony Gonzales hit a three-run home run on the next pitch, and when Bunning struck out the side in the ninth, the Mets had chalked up another in a long line of ingenious and, for a hard-luck pitcher like Stallard, frustrating losses.

For Stallard, as for many of those early Mets, one of the few good things about playing on such bad teams was the chance to get to know Casey Stengel. If anybody could find something humorous in a losing situation, it was Stengel. "As most baseball fans know, the Mets played their first two years in the old Polo Grounds in the Bronx," says Stallard. "And there was a train that ran in a loop around the ballpark. Well, in the first game I pitched for the Mets at the Polo Grounds in 1963, I got hammered. I gave up six or seven runs before I even got one out. Casey called time, walked out to the mound, and said, 'Larsen,'—he called every tall pitcher like me that he didn't know well "Larsen," after Don Larsen—'Larsen, if you hurry up and take a shower, you can catch that same train out of town that you came in on.'"

"In a game the following year, again at the Polo Grounds, I was pitching against the Phillies," Stallard recalls. "This was the year before they were going to raze the Polo Grounds because Shea Stadium would be ready for the 1965 season. The first two times Johnny Callison came up, he hit two rifles into the upper deck down the right-field line. They were both smoked, and you could hear the balls rattling and bouncing around in the seats. After the second one, Casey came out to the mound and said, 'Hey, young fella, how you doin'?'

"'Okay, I guess,' I said.

"'Well, just keep on doin' that, and there'll be one section up there they won't have to tear down next year.'"

DON SUTTON

When Hall of Fame pitcher Don Sutton was a kid growing up in Clio, Alabama, he and his mother had a running feud: Sutton loved the New York Yankees, but his mother loved the Brooklyn Dodgers. "As a youngster, I just couldn't imagine playing for any other team but the Yankees," says Sutton. "As I followed that team, I would think, 'Who wouldn't want to pitch for a team that had Ellie Howard and Yogi Berra catching and Mickey Mantle chasing down your mistakes in the outfield?'"

Despite Sutton's youthful allegiance to the Bronx Bombers, Mother Sutton had the last laugh when it came time for Don to sign his first professional baseball contract. Influenced by the Dodgers' emphasis on defense and pitching and impressed by the organization's unusual ability to develop outstanding pitchers, Sutton cast his fate with the Los Angeles Dodgers. It was a decision Sutton never regretted, as he picked up the first 233 of his 324 lifetime wins in a Dodgers uniform. Five years after he retired from baseball, while making his Hall of Fame acceptance speech, Sutton remembered his deceased mother and her allegiance to the Dodgers. "The only thing that could have made this day better," said Sutton, "was for my mother to be here. She would have been proud of me, but she'd have been even more excited to spend the weekend with Sandy Koufax. She loved watching Sandy Koufax pitch, and she loved the Los Angeles Dodgers."

As beautifully as things turned out between Sutton and the Dodgers, only the eccentricity of a certain owner kept Sutton from originally signing with a different team.

"Before I signed with the Dodgers, I had a handshake deal with Whitey Herzog to sign with the old Kansas City Athletics," says Sutton. "I was going to get a bonus of $17,500, the rest of my college education paid for, and a brand-new white Buick Riviera with red bucket seats. Whitey called Charlie Finley, the owner of the A's, to confirm the deal.

"Whitey handed me the phone, and Finley asked me, 'What's your nickname?'

" 'I don't have one,' I said.

"Finley said, 'Look, kid, I just signed Blue Moon [Odom], Jumbo Jim [Nash], and Catfish [Hunter]. If you don't have a nickname, I can't give you the money.'

"Whitey said, 'What'd he say? What'd he say?'

"I handed the phone back to him, and when he put the receiver up to his ear, the line was dead. And that was the end of my career with the Kansas City A's."

BIRDIE TEBBETTS

An All-Star major league catcher back in the 1940s, Birdie Tebbetts is now more remembered for his managing of the Reds, Braves, and Indians during the fifties and sixties than for his playing. Although he didn't know what to call it, Tebbetts was an early proponent of the science of psychocybernetics or positive self-imaging, as the following story illustrates.

In 1958, when Tebbetts was piloting the Reds, his everyday right fielder was Jerry Lynch, a good hitter but a liability as a fielder. On one very sunny day in Wrigley Field, Lynch stumbled around like a drunk and missed two fly balls, prompting an exasperated Tebbetts to say, "If Lynch would keep telling himself, 'I'm Tris Speaker, I'm Tris Speaker,' he might catch one of those fly balls. But he keeps telling himself, 'I'm Jerry Lynch, I'm Jerry Lynch.'"

Doc Edwards, a catcher on the 1963 Cleveland Indians squad managed by Tebbetts, remembers Tebbetts fondly as one of the most knowledgeable baseball men he ever met. Edwards says that Tebbetts was a great guy to play for but that he had a couple of strictly enforced rules.

"Birdie's first rule was that nobody was ever supposed to complain about the weather. You just weren't allowed to say it was too hot or too cold, and if you did you got fined. Birdie's thinking was that he didn't want you coming to the ballpark in a great frame of mind to play ball and having somebody give you a negative thought about how bad the weather was, because then you wouldn't want to go out and play.

"Well, one day we were in Kansas City, and it was a blisteringly hot day. One of our guys walked into the clubhouse before the game, and the first words out of his mouth were 'Aw, man, is it hot!' As soon as he said it, you could see it in his face that he remembered Birdie's rule, and sure enough, when he looked over his shoulder there was Birdie, who heard what he had said. So the guy added instantly, 'But that's just the way I like it!'

"Birdie's other rule was a ban on the 'MF' word. He just hated to hear it, and the fine for using it was a hundred dollars. Birdie even banned the abbreviated form of that obscenity, as in 'you mother.' The fine for that was fifty dollars. In 1966 Del Crandall spent the last year of his big league playing career with the Indians. The guy who had the foulest mouth on the team was the one who explained this rule to Crandall, and when he did, Crandall said, 'Well, hell, there goes your whole conversation!'"

FRANK THOMAS

For a decade and a half (1951–65) Frank Thomas was one of the leading power hitters in the National League. Altogether, Thomas cranked out 286 dingers, with a high of 35 in 1958 for the Pittsburgh Pirates and a heroic 34 in 1962 for the hapless first-year New York Mets. Although Thomas was also a defensive asset to his ball clubs for being capable of playing three positions (outfield, third, and first), he achieved his greatest notoriety "with the glove" for not using one—i.e., for catching anyone's hardest throw barehanded.

"I guess the barehanded thing started when I was a kid, playing fast-pitch softball in Pittsburgh," says Thomas. "My family couldn't afford to buy me a glove, so I played shortstop without one. Not having a glove taught me how to give with the ball, and I quickly developed real soft hands.

"The first time I ever challenged anybody was in the minor leagues in 1949. I was playing for Waco, Texas, and one day I was ribbing one of our pitchers, Bill Pierro, about how slow he threw. He tried to argue with me, so I told him I could catch his fastest pitch barehanded. When he accepted the challenge, I told him that I wanted him to go to the bullpen to warm up first, because if he didn't, after I caught his fastest pitch, he'd complain that he wasn't properly warmed up.

"Well, he didn't want to do that, so we stepped off sixty feet, six inches in the outfield, he wound up and fired his best fastball, and I caught it with my bare hands. Sure enough, he said, 'I wasn't warmed up!' So he went to the bullpen and got really warmed up. He came back to the outfield and threw five more fastballs, and I caught every one of them. And let me tell you, that really deflated his ego.

"After that, I did it all the time, and it was easy to find fish because major leaguers just aren't going to believe that anybody can catch their hardest throws without a glove. One day when I was with the Mets in 1962, we were playing the Giants. Richie Ashburn and I were warming up in front of our dugout when Willie Mays walked by. 'Hey, Willie,' said Ashburn, 'you want to make a quick hundred dollars? I'll bet you a C-note Frank can catch your hardest throw barehanded at sixty feet, six inches.'

" 'Like heck he can,' said Mays.

"I took off my glove and started catching Richie barehanded to warm up, and when Willie saw that he said, 'Let's make it five dollars.' So we did. We stepped off the distance, he threw his hardest, I caught it, and to this day Willie hasn't paid me yet.

"I never lost a challenge, but the guy who came the closest to beating me was Don Zimmer when we were both on the Chicago Cubs. Zimmer backed up ten yards, ran up to the sixty-foot line, and then threw me a spitter, but I still caught the ball. He threw his glove up in the air in exasperation and said, 'You've made a believer out of me!'

"I really had a lot of fun with the thing over the years. It isn't that hard a thing to do if you know how to catch the right way, and, as a matter of fact, I caught a lot of balls with my throwing hand in actual major league games. I had such soft hands that a glove was almost a hindrance to me."

DON POLLARD

LUIS TIANT

Like a lot of other pitchers, Luis Tiant had the best season of his career in 1968, the year when pitchers in both leagues dominated the hitters to an unprecedented extent. In "The Year of the Pitcher," for example, five American League starting pitchers finished with an ERA under 2.00; Detroit's Denny McLain become the majors' first 30-game winner since 1934; and Boston's Carl Yastrzemski captured the Junior Circuit's batting title with a batting average of only .301. As for Cleveland's cigar-smoking Cuban with the baffling corkscrew delivery, Tiant went 21–9 and led the league with nine shutouts and his microscopic 1.60 ERA. "Looie" also made his first All-Star team that year and, in fact, was picked by manager Dick Williams to start the game for the American League.

The thirty-ninth All-Star Game, which was played in Houston's Astrodome, followed the script for the 1968 season perfectly, as the National League won 1–0 with the two leagues combining for a total of only eight hits. The game was not only the first 1–0 decision in the history of the Midsummer Classic, but the lone run scored was appropriately an unearned run, and it came off of Luis Tiant.

Playing in place of the injured Pete Rose, Willie Mays led off the bottom of the first inning with a single to left field. As the speedy Mays took his lead off first base, Tiant snapped a throw to first baseman Harmon Killebrew of the Minnesota Twins. The surprised Killebrew missed the throw for an error—the ball actually hit him in the chest and rolled away—and Mays scampered down to second. While throwing ball four to Curt

Flood, the rattled Tiant uncorked a wild pitch that allowed Mays to advance to third. When Willie McCovey then grounded into a 4-6-3 double play (Rod Carew to Jim Fregosi to Killebrew), Mays crossed home plate with what turned out to be the only run of the game.

It was the sixth consecutive All-Star Game loss for the American Leaguers, none of whom were more disappointed than Tiant, who summed up the game by saying, "My first All-Star Game and I lose it 1–0. Why? Because I throw to first base to pick off Willie Mays. I pick off Killebrew instead."

TICKET SCALPING AND COUNTERFEITING

You may not like ticket scalpers, but you have to admit that they are pretty enterprising people, especially in Denver, Colorado, where the Rockies play at continually sold-out Coors Field. Ticket scalping in Denver is illegal, but in 1997 scalpers found an ingenious, if also galling, way around that little technicality. Denver scalpers would sell a Rockies ticket at face value but require the buyer to also purchase, as part of the same transaction, a common player baseball card, worth a few pennies, for an additional $50.

Ticket scalping reached an even more ridiculous extreme during the 1996 World Series in New York. Taking advantage of New York fans' desperation to see their first World Series in Yankee Stadium in fifteen years, scalpers demanded and received up to $2,000 for one $70 ticket. New York City Consumer Affairs Commissioner Jose Maldonado actually cited and fined ten ticket agencies for unfairly overcharging. If such price gouging weren't bad enough, fans also had to contend with counterfeit ticket rings who produced high-quality fakes.

The ersatz World Series ducats were not perfect by any means. They were printed on thinner stock than the real tickets, were not as vividly colored, and lacked a Major League Baseball watermark logo that was visible only in ultraviolet light. These defects were not apparent, though, to fans who did not have real tickets to compare them to, and many unsuspecting fans were fooled. One such victim was a man named Charlie Hernandez—ironically, a photocopy machine operator by trade—who shelled out $1,000 for seven counterfeit tickets to Games 1 and 2. Hernandez's simple, sad reaction to his blunder: "I was a sucker."

UMPIRES

At one time the American League required team managers to rank the league's umpires from 1 to 64 as a way of evaluating its arbiters. Many umpires objected to such a system because of its subjective nature, the potential for poor ratings due to managerial grudges, and the unfairness of imposing distinctions among all umpires when many were equal in ability and performance.

Of all people, it was legendary umpire baiter Billy Martin who recognized the innate unfairness of the system. Martin, who at various times managed the Twins, Tigers, Rangers, Yankees, and Athletics, lodged a tacit protest against the system by always ranking all umpires the same. Every year he ranked all sixty-four umpires No. 1.

As the Men in Blue like to say, "Umpiring is the only occupation in the world where you're expected to be perfect the first day on the job and then improve every day after that." Yes, umpiring is a tough job, particularly in the minor leagues, where the overall conditions and two- and three-man crews compound the difficulties. Minor league umpire Joe Zureick recalls an incident from his rookie season in professional baseball in 1970 that illustrates this point.

"I was assigned to the Appalachian League," says Zureick, "and my partner and I were doing a night game between the Johnson City Yankees and the Marion Mets in Johnson City, Tennessee. It was late in the game, and the Mets were batting. They had a runner on first base, and since I was doing the bases I was positioned between first and second. The batter hit a long line drive that was going over the head of the Yankees' center fielder. As the center fielder was going back on the ball, he blocked my view. To make things worse, it was really foggy, and the lights were bad to begin with. With the fog, the bad lighting, and the bad angle I had, I couldn't tell what happened on the play. I looked back to my partner, the home-plate umpire, for help. He was making the home-run sign, circling his hand over his head, so I went with him and started making the same sign.

"The only problem is that we got it wrong. The PA announcer saw what had happened because he was sitting up high in the press box, so he shouted over the PA system, "Mr. Umpire, that ball bounced over the fence!" In those days the PA announcers took a lot of liberties they don't dare take nowadays. The Yankees screamed and hollered about it, but we didn't change the call because there was nobody else for my partner and me to confer with. Of course, the Yankees lost the game, so the Yankees and the Johnson City fans weren't very happy with us. After the game we got out of there in a hurry.

"Now, the league was based in Bristol, Tennessee. The league president lived there, and all the umpires stayed in the same hotel, the Hotel Bristol. You roomed with your partner, and it was four dollars per night per man. This had all been arranged by the league president. Well, after we got back to Bristol, my partner and I stayed up until the Johnson City newspapers hit the newsstands. He went to one of them, and I went to the other, and together we bought all the Johnson City papers, so that the league president and the other umpires wouldn't be able to read about our screwup the night before. It was a forgone conclusion that the Johnson City newspaper would rip us good, and they did. We knew the league president would eventually find out; we just didn't want him to find out that day. We wanted some time to think up a story to tell him.

"Our little scheme wasn't successful, but things worked out okay anyway. Somehow the league president did find out about the game that day, but he just laughed about it when he talked to us. And for some reason the Johnson City Yankees never brought it up again. We really got off easy."

Zureick also remembers how a common inconvenience of minor league umpiring made him privy to an amusing phone call.

"When minor league ballparks are built, they never seem to remember to build dressing facilities for the umpires, so the umpires often have to dress in the general manager's office. One day we were going to do a game in Marion, Virginia, and I was getting dressed in the Mets' GM's office.

"The GM was in his office, along with Jerry Lumpe, the Mets' batting coach; Chuck Estrada, the pitching coach; and Whitey Herzog, the Mets' manager. Lumpe, Estrada, and Herzog had all had nice major league playing careers, and Whitey of course went on to become a very successful major league manager.

"The GM was on the phone, and I heard him talking: 'Sure, sure. We're very interested in you. You want $14,500 to play the season and a bonus of $18,500 to sign a contract . . . that's a total of $33,000. What? You want a total of $43,000? Okay. No problem. What's another $10,000?'

"I realized that the GM was talking to a hot prospect, and I thought the Mets must really want the guy, because when the GM got finished talking to the guy, he had everybody else in the room talk to him too. Lumpe talked to him, then Estrada talked to him, and finally Herzog talked to him. Herzog asked him things like 'Are you in shape? Have you been working out?'

"I was really impressed, so after Herzog hung the phone up, I asked him, 'Whitey, what in the heck was that all about?'

"'Aw, nothing,' said Herzog. 'That guy calls every week. He lives down the street in a home for the criminally insane.'"

MO VAUGHN

Anaheim Angels first baseman Mo Vaughn is a huge, menacing presence in the batter's box. The mere sight of Vaughn swishing his bat back and forth is enough to send chills down the spines of most pitchers. All Mo has to do to prove his toughness, though, is roll up the sleeve of his shirt.

You see, Vaughn liked his college fraternity at Seton Hall so much that he decided to make an indelible impression of Omega Psi Phi on . . . himself.

He fashioned interlocking Greek omega symbols out of a coat hanger, heated the coat hanger in boiling olive oil, and then branded the omegas into his right bicep. Ouch!

I guess an embroidered sweater was out of the question.

ROBIN VENTURA

Don't be surprised if Chicago White Sox players cringe every time they hear the phrase "breaks of the game"—not after what happened to their teammate Robin Ventura in a 1997 spring training game.

With Chicago hosting the Boston Red Sox in Sarasota, Florida, Ventura was on second base with two outs in the fourth inning when Ray Durham singled to left field. The White Sox's All-Star third baseman tried to score on the play, but when he slid into home, the spikes on his right shoe caught on the plate and his foot crumpled underneath him. Ventura suffered not only a dislocated ankle but also a double fracture to his tibia and fibula. Even worse, one of the broken bones was a compound fracture, which means the bone broke through the skin.

The injury was such a gruesome sight that it caused another injury requiring medical attention when a woman in the box seats fainted and cracked her head on the concrete floor of the grandstands. Television sportscasters also warned their audiences before showing videotape of the horrible accident.

Ventura's wife, visibly shaken, went onto the field but was steered away from her fallen husband by White Sox personnel, who also shielded her view.

White Sox players turned away quickly after catching just a glimpse of Ventura's injuries, and some of them, such as shortstop Ozzie Guillen, wouldn't look at all. "I saw guys wave to the dugout, but I didn't want to see it. I didn't have the guts to see it. I feel more sick now than I felt with my own injury," said Guillen, referring to the time he hyperextended his knee in 1992 when he collided with an outfielder.

White Sox team doctor James Boscardin relocated Ventura's ankle in the clubhouse training room, and then Ventura was taken to Sarasota Memorial Hospital, where he was operated on until four in the morning. Boscardin said he'd seen worse but admitted that there was a lot of damage to Ventura's leg.

Amazingly, Ventura not only made a full recovery but also returned in time to play part of the 1997 season, missing only the team's first ninety-nine games. While he was recovering, Ventura received a tremendous volume of get-well mail from White Sox fans. This touched him so much that the following year he bought fifteen of his own White Sox jerseys, autographed them, and gave one away to a lucky fan after every White Sox home-stand.

DON POLLARD

DAVID WELLS

When New York Yankees owner George Steinbrenner signed pitcher David Wells to a three-year, $13.5-million-dollar, free-agent contract prior to the 1997 season, Steinbrenner knew he wasn't getting the prototypical Yankee. Wells's pierced ear, the tattoos on his chest and shoulder, his penchant for playing loud heavy-metal rock music in the clubhouse, and the Hell's Angels motorcycle gang members he counted among his friends were all things that didn't exactly fit the classy, conservative Yankees mold. Nor did Wells improve his image when he broke his hand in a street brawl outside a bar in Ocean Beach, California, shortly after he signed the big contract.

The irony of this apparent mismatch was the fact that Wells considered playing for the Yankees a dream come true because as a boy he had idolized Babe Ruth. "I admire the way he saved the game following the 1919 'Black Sox' scandal," says Wells. "From everything I've read and heard, he was fun to watch and he was a hero to a lot of people. That's why I always did reports on him when I was in school." Wells showed how serious his affection for the Babe is when he purchased an authentic Ruth Yankees cap for $35,000 at a 1997 auction. Wells's teammates and Yankees manager Joe Torre could live with that, but not with Wells's decision to wear the cap while pitching in an actual game. "Joe told me to take it off," says Wells. "He wasn't too happy about it, but that's understandable. I was only going to wear it for one inning."

While the Ruth-cap stunt confirmed his status as a flake, the thing about Wells that really bugged Torre and Steinbrenner was his weight. Wells not only cherishes the Ruthian legend, but at 250-plus pounds he also resembles the Babe . . . at least around the waist. Wells's spare tire (as was the Babe's) is caused at least in part by his fondness for frothy adult beverages. Unlike Torre and Steinbrenner, Yankee fans have been able to find some humor in this. On a sweltering July day in 1997, Wells was pitching a good game against the Oakland A's at Yankee Stadium. While mopping the sweat from his brow, Wells looked up and noticed fans in the upper deck keeping a running tabulation of his strikeouts, not in the usual way by hanging on a railing placards with the letter "K" (the traditional symbol for a strikeout), but by hanging placards with pictures of frosty beer mugs! Wells pitched so well that day that he set a personal record for strikeouts with sixteen. The fans hanging the beer mug pictures ran out of cards after Wells's eleventh, so they improvised after that and hung up empty beer cups. Wells laughed when he saw the placards, later complimented the fans on their sense of humor and creativity, and added, "I could have used a beer myself. I was getting pooped out there."

Complaints about his weight followed Wells into the 1998 season. On May 6, he gave up seven runs to the Texas Rangers in two innings, and Joe Torre clearly alluded to his hefty lefty's extra poundage when he said that Wells "ran out of gas." Eleven days later, though, Wells made Torre eat those words by pitching a 4–0 perfect game against the Minnesota Twins in New York. In notching only the thirteenth perfect game in major league history since 1900, Wells struck out eleven and survived only one real scare, a scorching grounder up the middle that second baseman Chuck Knoblauch had to knock down backhanded. After Wells retired number twenty-seven in a row (Pat Meares on a fly ball to right), he received the traditional ride off the field on the shoulders of his teammates. So what if it took three players, not two, to hoist Wells off the ground? As Wells himself said, "To pitch a perfect game wearing pinstripes at Yankee Stadium, it's unbelievable. Growing up a Yankee fan, to come out here and make history, it really is a dream come true." In throwing his perfecto, Wells didn't permanently defuse the issue of his bulging waistline, but he did prove that he wasn't a total misfit in a Yankees uniform. After all, didn't the Yankees adopt pinstripes in the first place to make Babe Ruth look thinner than he really was?

TURK WENDELL

New York Mets fans may be happy with the solid relief pitching of Turk Wendell, but they aren't getting even half of the entertainment that Wendell provided baseball fans in Des Moines during his two-year-plus association with the Triple-A Iowa Cubs. Wendell, you see, had a host of most unusual habits that he was allowed to indulge when he pitched in the minors for the Cubs. These habits, which became known as "Turk's Quirks," endeared him to Iowa Cubs fans, but they were virtually outlawed by the image-conscious conformity police of the Chicago Cubs, who told Turk "to tone it down" once he reached the big leagues.

What exactly were these "Turk's Quirks" that major league fans are missing?

Well, in the minors Turk used to jump high over the baseline in a "leap of faith" as he went out to the mound.

He chewed black licorice instead of tobacco—he'd put three sticks of it in his mouth before heading to the mound each inning.

Because the licorice turned his teeth black, he would brush his teeth right in the dugout between innings.

A sincere Christian, Wendell would trace three crosses in the dirt of the pitcher's mound and say a little prayer facing center field before the start of each inning.

He also would wave to the center fielder, who had to wave back before Turk would turn around and face home plate (this was a carryover of something Turk and his best friend in high school used to do). Actually, sometimes the center fielder wouldn't wave back, in which case Turk would wave to the right fielder, then the left fielder, et cetera, until somebody did wave back.

If his catcher was standing, Turk would squat and not stand up until the catcher went into his squatting position.

Turk would never take a throw from the umpire, only from one of his teammates. If the umpire did throw him a baseball, Turk would step aside, let the ball hit the ground, and require a teammate to pick it up and toss it to him.

Prior to brushing his teeth between innings, Turk would also wrap up his pitching arm like a mummy in his "funny" towel.

Turk wore only stirrup socks—never any sanitaries, the long white stockings that ballplayers normally wear underneath their stirrups—and he adopted 13 as his lucky number.

Rather than repress Wendell's personality, the Iowa Cubs allowed Turk to give his eccentricities free rein. Group sales director Nick Willey, moreover, was quick to seize upon their marketing and promotional value. Willey hired a local artist to execute a drawing of Wendell for a "Turk's Quirks" T-shirt, which illustrated and described ten of the quirks. The shirts were an instant hit: the I-Cubs' gift shop sold out the initial order of twelve dozen shirts the very first night they were offered and took advance orders for six dozen more. The shirts, logically priced at $13 each, remained the gift shop's best-selling item for the duration of Turk's reign in Iowa.

Skeptics suggested that the quirks were an act put on by an egomaniac starved for attention, but those who knew Wendell firsthand insisted that, on the contrary, he was one of the most genuine, down-to-earth persons anyone could hope to meet. "Turk was probably the friendliest, most sincere player we've ever had here," says Willey. "Certainly, he's the most popular player we've ever had. He was especially great with the kids. He'd sign autographs for hours at a time, let kids run with him in the outfield, and even take them fishing. I don't know any other player who'd do those things."

Turk Wendell may be a flake, but it is extremely doubtful that he is a fake. This is something Willey realized from his very first meeting with Wendell. "There's a one-room log cabin built in 1843 that sits in the corner of our parking lot," says Willey. "As the first dwelling to be built in Des Moines, it represents the founding of the city. Turk said, 'I want to live there. It's close to the ballpark.' I told him, 'You can't live there; it's a historical monument. Besides, it doesn't have any water or electricity.' Turk accepted that explanation, and he wound up living in the home of some local people, with whom he has become very good friends, but can you imagine such a crazy idea even occurring to anybody else?"

TED WILLIAMS

The last man to hit .400 over an entire major league season, Ted Williams is considered by many to be the greatest hitter who ever lived. Williams was certainly one of the game's great characters, and it seems that everybody who ever played with or against him has at least one Teddy Ballgame story. Pitcher Mel Parnell, who played his entire ten-year career with Ted on the Red Sox, tells the following tale about the cocky, proud perfectionist who terrorized American League hurlers for nineteen years.

"We were playing Washington one day, and Pedro Ramos happened to strike Ted out. When Ramos got the ball back from the catcher, he carefully tossed it into the Senators' dugout so that he could keep the ball as a souvenir. After the game, Ramos came over into our clubhouse, walked up to Ted's locker, and asked Ted to sign the ball.

"Well, Ted got mad. He scowled at Ramos and said, 'Get the hell out of here! I'm not signing any ball I struck out on.'

"Ramos started begging Ted to sign the ball, but Ted was still cussing him out. Ramos was just a kid at the time, and he almost started crying, but he wouldn't give up. Finally, Ted could see that Pedro was sincere, so he took the ball and signed it. But he wasn't happy about it.

"About a month later we were playing Washington again. Ramos was pitching again, and this time Ted hit one a mile off him that went way up into the upper deck. Ted trotted around the bases, and as he hit the third-base bag he suddenly remembered Ramos. He looked toward Ramos on the pitching mound and yelled, 'Get that son of a bitch back and I'll sign it too!'"

It wasn't only the fans who were amazed by Ted Williams's ability to hit a baseball. Opposing players and his own team-mates were just as astonished. Hall of Fame second baseman Bobby Doerr, who was a longtime friend and teammate of Williams, says that one reason Ted was such a great hitter is that he was constantly looking for any little edge that he could take advantage of.

"When Ted was a young guy, he always went to the good hitters and asked them for advice," says Doerr. "In 1938 he asked Rogers Hornsby in Minneapolis what he had to do to become a good hitter. Hornsby told him, 'Ted, to be a great hitter, you have to stay in the strike zone.' Ted never forgot that, and in fact he made that the number-one tenet of his own phi-losophy of hitting. Later on Ted got criticized for not swinging at pitches a little out of the strike zone when we needed a ball to be put in play—maybe a fly ball to score a run from third—but Ted would say, 'No, I'm not going to do it, because it'll lead to bad habits.' Without a doubt, Ted was the most disciplined hitter I ever saw.

"Ted also had the most intense concentration at the plate of anybody I ever saw. I remember one time we were playing in the afternoon and Ted was batting. A little cloud came over-head and darkened just the area of home plate where Ted was hitting. He backed out and waited for the cloud to move. Ninety-nine percent of us wouldn't even have noticed the cloud, but it was enough to distract Ted.

"And then there was the time we had an exhibition game in Louisville, Kentucky, that we were going to play on our way back north at the end of spring training. Ted wanted to visit the Hillerich & Bradsby bat factory before we played that afternoon, so we went over there at seven o'clock in the morning. We had to sit on the steps and wait half an hour for the place to open. As soon as it did, Ted made a beeline for the lathe area where the bat makers turn the bats. Ted liked billets that had a lot of pin knots in them—he thought pin knots made for a stronger bat—so he told one of the bat makers, 'When you get a billet that has a lot of those little knots in it, I want you to make one of my bats out of it.' And then Ted gave the guy twenty dollars, which was a very big tip in those days. Like I said, Ted took advantage of every little thing he could, and when it came to hitting there was nothing so insignificant that it was beneath his notice."

DON YOUNG

Despite a brief and relatively insignificant major league career, former Chicago Cubs outfielder Don Young became a legend of sorts, a mystery man whose disappearance was attributed to shame and bitterness. Here's how the legend was created and what the truth turned out to be.

The 1969 Chicago Cubs are remembered as one of baseball history's most underachieving great teams. The club's failure to win the National League Eastern Division title was an especially titanic disappointment for long-suffering Cubs fans who thought that their team, led by stars Ernie Banks, Billy Williams, Ron Santo, Ferguson Jenkins, and manager Leo Durocher, finally had the right stuff. After the Cubs blew an early-August eight-and-a-half-game lead and lost the pennant by dropping eight in a row and eleven of twelve at the start of September, the finger-pointing and recriminations flew.

On July 8 the Cubs lost a one-run game at Shea Stadium to the New York Mets, the team that eventually beat Chicago out of the pennant. Directly contributing to the loss were two ninth-inning plays involving rookie center fielder Don Young. On the first play Young broke back on a soft catchable liner that fell in for a hit, and on the second he dropped what was ruled a double after he ran into the outfield wall. After the game in the Cubs' clubhouse, manager Durocher and third baseman Santo furiously berated Young for what they considered to be errors, and the next day Durocher replaced Young in the starting lineup with Jim Qualls. It was only one loss in the middle of the season, but the game later came to symbolize the team's collapse and its inability to deal with adversity.

As for Young, the incident virtually ended his baseball career. Young was a "good field–no hit" type of player who had made the Cubs in '69 by default: because regular center fielder Adolfo Phillips had been injured and because a couple of more talented prospects had not panned out in the spring. Although Young had fielded his position more than competently prior to the game on July 8, Durocher lost confidence in him after that. Young played sparingly the rest of 1969 and was unceremoniously sold to a minor league team by Durocher at the end of spring training the following year. A year and a half later, the discouraged Young quit professional baseball.

Away from baseball, Young bounced around the western United States, working at a variety of low-paying jobs and making no attempt whatsoever to keep in touch with his old teammates. As time went by, the pain of the Cubs' unsuccessful 1969 campaign was alleviated by the salve of nostalgia, and the players began to be viewed as the glorious "lost cause" heroes of Cubs history. Players from the '69 Cubs' roster often made paid appearances to sign autographs at baseball card shows, but Don Young was never among them, primarily because no one, it seemed, had any idea where Don Young was. Rumors began circulating that Young had intentionally withdrawn from baseball society because he was mad at Santo and Durocher and because he still felt the humiliation of having been branded a real-life Charlie Brown.

The image of Don Young as the brooding hermit was solidified in 1989 when Rick Talley published a book called *The Cubs of '69: Recollections of the Team That Should Have Been*. Talley interviewed every member of the team for the book except Don Young. In fact, a large part of Talley's chapter on Young is devoted to an account of the various last known whereabouts of Young, as well as Talley's own exhaustive and futile efforts to locate the former Cub.

Although Talley could not find Young, he did learn from others that Young had always been a loner and that he had long before forgiven Santo, who after all had apologized to Young in front of the entire Cubs team the day after Santo's tirade. These facts tended to contradict the notion that Young was hiding, yet the book, which was published by a major publisher, did not bring Young out of obscurity.

In 1992 a card show reunion of the '69 Cubs was being planned for the fall. Chicago veterinarian Rich Nye, who had been a pitcher on the team, spent a lot of time RSVPing his former teammates for the reunion, but he had given up trying to find Young. Then one day an affable elderly lady with a sick bird called on Dr. Nye. Noticing the Cubs memorabilia in Nye's office, she asked if Nye had played for the Cubs. When Nye said that he had, the lady said that she had a relative who had played for the Cubs too: Don Young. Nye could hardly believe what he was hearing, and he was delighted to learn from the old woman how to finally get ahold of Young.

As it turned out, Young was not hiding from the past at all. He had simply gotten on with his life after baseball. He showed up for the reunion in November 1992, and his appearance was considered one of the highlights of the event. When asked why he'd never before returned to Chicago, he said, "First of all, I had no idea people were looking for me. Second, I had no idea players could make so much money from just signing their names. If I had known how things were going to turn out, I would have come back a lot sooner."

INDEX

233

McNall, Bruce, 41
McNamara, John, 99, 100
Meares, Pat, 216
Melton, Bill, 96
Memorabilia, 40–50
Memorial Stadium, 10, 11, 22
Menke, Denis, 94
Metro, Charlie, 128–29
Mexican League, 115–17
Michaels, Al, 97
Miller, Orlando, 177
Minor leagues, 120–29
Miranda, Willie, 47
Mizell, Wilmer David, 130–31
Molay, Steve, 50
Monbouquette, Bill, 21
Mondale, Walter, 30
Montague, Ed, 177
Montefusco, John, 132–34
Morales, Jerry, 135–36
Morgan, Mike, 139
Mosser, Tom, 112
Municipal Stadium, 95
Munson, Thurman, 137–40
Murakami, Masanori, 141
Murcer, Bobby, 139
Murphy, Mike, 23, 33
Murray, Eddie, 43, 44
Murtaugh, Danny, 37, 54
Musial, Stan, 47

Nastu, Phil, 23

Nettles, Graig, 140
Neville, Tim, 12–15
New York Mets, 25, 75–76, 80–81, 135–36, 139, 152–54, 194–95
New York Yankees, 3–5, 7–8, 10, 47–48, 137–40, 143, 215–17. *See also* Gehrig, Lou; Mantle, Mickey; Ruth, Babe
Newsom, Bobo, 88, 146–48
Niekro, Phil, 149–51
Nomo, Hideo, 141
Nordhagen, Wayne, 95
Norman, Freddie, 25, 26
Northrup, Jim, 192
Numbers, players', 143–45
Nunn, Howie, 142
Nye, Rich, 228

O'Donnell, Joe, 63, 65
O'Donnell, Pat, 63–65
Oh, Sadaharu, 45
Ojeda, Bob, 164
Olin, Steve, 162, 164, 165
Olympic Stadium, 185
O'Neill, Kelly, 118–19
Otto, Dave, 142
Oyler, Ray, 192

Pacella, John, 135, 137, 139–40, 152–59
Paige, Satchel, 88, 89